Established as an all-round entertainer, *Colette Mann* has been delighting Australian audiences with her inimitable style for many years in all areas of television, radio and film.

Born in Canada too many years ago, *Annie Page* now lives in Australia. She has spent the past decade working as a publicist in Sydney and befriending local megastars.

COLETTE MANN
WITH ANNIE PAGE

It's a Mann's World

WELDON
PUBLISHING

SYDNEY · HONG KONG · CHICAGO · LONDON

A Kevin Weldon Production
Published by Weldon Publishing
a division of Kevin Weldon & Associates Pty Limited
372 Eastern Valley Way, Willoughby, NSW 2068, Australia

First published 1990

© Copyright text: Colette Mann and Annie Page 1990
© Copyright design and illustrations: Kevin Weldon & Associates Pty Limited 1990

Editor: Jill Wayment
Designer: Michele Withers
Cartoonist: Kerry Millard
Typeset in 11.5 pt Palatino by Midland Typesetters, Maryborough, Victoria
Printed in Australia by The Book Printer, Maryborough, Victoria

National Library of Australia Cataloguing-in-Publication data

Mann, Colette (Colette Janine).
   It's a Mann's world: a random guide to life as it is—
coming to grips with surviving in the 1990s.
   ISBN 1 86302 111 6.
   1. Australian wit and humor.
   I. Page, Annie. II. Title.

A828.307

All rights reserved. Subject to the Copyright Act 1968, no part
of this publication may be reproduced, stored in a retrieval
system, or transmitted in any form or by any means, electronic,
mechanical, photocopying, recording, or otherwise, without
the prior written permission of the publisher.

This book is printed on partly recycled paper.

Contents

How two nice girls like us found
ourselves writing a book like this *1*

1 / Milestones or millstones
Turning forty and other burdens 5

2 / How to cope when your friends think
your morning sickness should be over
by midday
Pregnancy and all its joys... 8

3 / Parenting—This century's greatest lie............. *14*

4 / 'Mrs, Mrs, come quickly...'
A renovator's sentimental journey 20

5 / Mothers, fathers, ageing aunties, hippie
sisters and partners' ex-partners
Solving the problem of the Sunday roast 26

6 / Santa doesn't stop here any more................ 29

7 / Weddings, parties... anything
*How to behave at a function when you'd
rather be somewhere else*..34

8 / How to survive when your trolley of
emotional baggage has a dicky wheel............. 37

9 / Uh-oh, look who's parting his hair on
the other side
The dead giveaways of male menopause....................42

10 / You picked a fine time to leave me,
you heel!
The agony and the ecstasy of divorce 45

11 / How to survive that abandoned feeling.......... 49
12 / Your best friend marries a dickhead—
Handle it!.. 50
13 / It's in, it's out, it's happening, it's not
Fads for foods, frills, fixes and fun........................... 54
14 / Travel in the nineties—
Exploding the myth... 60
15 / A salute to cellulite—Phasing fat into fit
Gym—I'd rather be eating cake!............................. 65
16 / The voting game
Who wins: them or us?... 69
17 / Causes for the nineties—
A list, but it's ours.. 76
18 / You oughta be congratulated.
They said you'd never make it . . .
Advertising—Oh, what a feeling!............................. 81
19 / Recycling our lives
'Who's looking after Planet Earth?'—
An alien's report... 89
20 / Give way to the right—
It may be your mother
Driving: a woman's view.. 96
21 / The ever-changing face of functions
A partygiver's guide to gracious gaiety.................... 101
22 / Out to shop!
Everything you ever wanted to know about
shopping but were afraid to ask............................. 105
23 / Not so much bankrupt as a little
financially embarrassed
Women—The real financiers of the nineties............... 110

24 / If you're going to stick it out, girls, then firm it up!
The corporate handshake—An introduction to a new career *114*

25 / When your software becomes floppy and your mouse has lost its byte
Surviving the technological age *117*

26 / Love in the suds
Soap opera junkies and proud of it *122*

27 / Are you ripe for sex in the nineties?
A comprehensive quiz to help assess your sensuality *131*

28 / The Nineties Woman
Now let's see who's been paying attention! *137*

29 / A survival register
What every Nineties Woman needs to have on hand *139*

Our Personal Acknowledgments

The authors would like to thank John Hall and Colin Fletcher for providing them with food and shelter during the creation of this tome; Jane Curry at Weldon for recognising exceptional talent when it was forced upon her; Dean Wallace of Body By Design for keeping the creators in top physical condition; Emma McCormack for the long hours she spent entertaining the sprog; and Chambers Thesaurus for its inspiration.

And, to all of those friends, relatives, acquaintances and National Treasures who may recognise something they have said in some way, at some time, in some place—we thank you for your invaluable contribution, whether you were aware that you were volunteering it or not: Anon; Milton Berle; Jane Cameron; Audrey Challinor; Ron Challinor; Joan Crawford; Salvador Dali; the Darling Harbour Aquarium; Dr Ruth; Kat Fox; Peter Garrett; Jane Griffin; Alex Hall; Rhyss Hall; Susan Humphrey; Josie, the greengrocer's wife; the Judge; Marion Landau; Norman Mailer; Mona Mann; Sue McIntosh; the Melbourne Zoo; Martha Page; Sue Parker; the Prime Minister of Australia; Lyn Tyack; David Webb; Henny Youngman.

If anyone has been left off this list, the authors would like it known that no correspondence will be entered into. We are very busy women and we cannot be expected to remember who said everything we have ever overheard!

How two nice girls like us found ourselves writing a book like this

We were tired, we were listless, we were bored with life. We discussed almost daily the need for a career change. We did have a few ideas—it wasn't just talk.

We seriously considered Dial-a-Pizza-and-a-Video until we got into a terrible kerfuffle over who was going to fling the dough and who was going to collect the video. A shop exclusively stocking clothes with elasticised waists was a real possibility for a while until we decided to go on a diet together instead. Our final choice of any significance was to start a therapeutic practice as sex surrogates, until we discovered exactly what it is they do that is so therapeutic.

With all this behind us—and nothing in front of us—we turned our investigative eyes to the world of high-class literature. It couldn't be too hard. We'd read a few books in our time. So that was it; we were on our way! Writing would be the new career for us.

Annie, being the more pragmatic of the two of us, was appointed to the position of Official Organiser in Charge of Career Change. Colette, being the less pragmatic of the two of us and pregnant, was asked to keep her mouth shut and to do as she was told.

Then, one day, while Annie was enthusiastically restacking the shelves of her newly renovated pantry for the third time, The Idea came to her. The huge, international, and incredibly entrepreneurial publishing house Weldon was approached, and as luck would have it for our heroines, they showed enormous interest in this project.

Annie was thrilled by her progress and was soon champing at the bit. Colette, suffering yet another bout of morning sickness, was agreeable to anything—luckily for Annie.

So now all that was left to do was to write the thing!

Obviously, writing a book together wasn't meant to be easy. We were immediately bowled over by a number of problems, not the least of which was the logistics of Annie living in Sydney and Colette living in Melbourne. Faxes and phones were running hot until Telecom declared its annual profit and we got the bill. Suffice it to say, the Hume Highway became as familiar to both of us as the floor plan of David Jones.

Once together physically, it was still a bit of a struggle. Quite frankly, not even the consumptive Brontë sisters on the English moors had to suffer what we endured for the creation of this work. Perhaps the fact that we spent a lot of time chatting and laughing (for research, of course) gave people the wrong impression. Our spouses, in particular, seemed to have a hard time understanding that we were actually *working* and not just having one of our usual days of girlie activity.

Apart from the normal day-to-day interruptions of telephones ringing for them, them ringing us on the telephone, couriers collecting and delivering for them, and 'What's for tea?', our partners had some other distractions in store for us.

Home maintenance became a very popular pastime for the boys during the writing of this epic. Handyman jobs that we had been so nicely requesting them to do for years suddenly became the most urgent tasks on their agenda. We guess it was just our bad luck that these chores proved to be so noisy and were situated so near to our place of writing.

There is nothing quite like going with the flow of a highly creative stream of thought only to have it punctuated by the clanging and banging of the central heating system being repaired, or the incessant scratching and scraping of old paint being removed from a window frame. But we ploughed on!

The only person who appeared at all sensitive to our artistic needs was Emma McCormack, nanny to young Sam Hall. She, too, became one with the Hume Highway, and we secretly suspect she is now compiling a handbook on diversions and distractions for toddlers of working mothers. On the very odd occasion when Sam did burst through the barricades into our garret of inspiration, we could count on Emma to be just a step behind. Added to this, she was invaluable in keeping us up-to-date with our favourite soap operas.

No great achievement is accomplished without tragedy and this one is no exception. Annie's cat, Pudda, much loved by all those fortunate enough to know him, passed away to Pussy's Heaven during the final stages of this work. Ironically, he had just mastered the art of using his newly renovated pussy door. Admittedly, his education was accelerated by being chased relentlessly by young Sam Hall. *Vale* Pudda, our thoughts are with you!

On top of all these complications, there was also Colette's schoolmarmish insistence that we start every day working out at the gym with Dean Wallace, her personal fitness trainer. (Annie has never experienced pain like it!) The wordsmiths were also regularly interrupted by Colette's trips to various members of the medical profession, as she clutched her urinary specimens and had her blood tested constantly. These disturbances were nothing compared to the endless stream of friends telephoning to ask, 'Am I in it?'

So all that's left, dear reader, is a word to explain the excellent but sometimes confusing style of the writing. As you read, it will become clear to you that some of the chapters have been written from first-hand experience—Colette's to be exact. So wherever you see 'I', it means her and wherever you see 'we', it means both of us, or the world in general.

Amazingly enough, we have survived this experience with our friendship and our senses of humour intact. But if we don't finish this paragraph soon, Annie's going to hit Colette over the head...

1

Milestones or millstones
Turning forty and other burdens

All of our lives we spend looking forward to the next milestone. Can you remember what it was like back in those heady days of being nine years old, just desperate to hit the big double figures? Well, ten comes and goes and then you suddenly find yourself at the ripe old age of twelve, hungering to be a teenager AND to wear your first bra.

To be honest, in my particular case, this order was reversed... just seconds after my *eleventh*(!) birthday, I found myself being pressed by my slightly hysterical mother into a 34B cup... (I completely bypassed 32A through to D).

Turning eighteen was fairly exciting because it meant you could drive a car, even if you didn't have one. Then the next three years waiting for The Big One seemed endless.

Twenty-one was Mecca. All would come right at twenty-one. One would be able to cope with any crisis, one's skin would certainly clear up and, in most cases in the early seventies, one would 'be allowed' to leave home.

I hasten to add that this was another order which was reversed in my life—I finally threw off the shackles of the family home at the age of twenty-three years and seven months, to be precise. Needless to say, I was a very late bloomer.

Marriage is a pretty big milestone—and for some it is a millstone of no mean proportion, too. But, to be brutally honest, the almost insurmountable milestone for me was twenty-nine.

'Excuse me!' I hear you cry. Whoever heard of *twenty-nine* being a problem? Well, everyone to his or her own signpost! Think about it. Twenty-nine has a particularly nasty ring to it. In my case, the horror was induced by a combination of the prospect of turning thirty, dealing with a marked change in my career, and discovering that my *Bride's Cookbook for Two* was no longer applicable to my life.

Thirty-five has been known to be an ugly time for some, possibly because it is exactly halfway through the biblical limit on the old 'three score and ten'.

But with all of these markers behind us, nothing looms larger than *The Big Four-Oh*. It is the age we remember our mothers being... at a time when it seemed inconceivable that we could ever be *that* old. It is the age that newspapers and magazines start to describe people as being 'middle-aged'. And tragically, for most of us, it means we are closer to the end than we are to the beginning.

Having faced all these inevitabilities, I also found that I was almost deafened by the ticking of my biological clock. 'Will I or won't I?', 'Time's running out!', 'Who will look after me in my old age?', and various other ridiculous reasons for taking on motherhood in the middle years, worked their way into my psyche.

So, luckily, today, one doesn't really have time to

ponder the intricacies of being forty, one is far too busy dealing with still more career changes... those of mother, co-author and superwoman.

2

*H*ow to cope when your friends think your morning sickness should be over by midday

Pregnancy and all its joys

Trying to decide just how to attack this chapter on pregnancy, I found myself thumbing through *The Concise English Dictionary* and guess what I found? The real meaning of the word 'pregnant' is 'fruitful, big (with consequences, etc.), implying more than is expressed'. You can say that again, Mr Concise!

Being a very career-oriented animal, I never really saw myself as the mothering sort. I can remember as far back as my teen years when all my girlfriends were talking about getting married and naming their children. I used to sit there and secretly think what boring bimbos they were.

But something really strange happened to me just after my thirty-seventh birthday. I went to the doctor assuming that my blood pressure was acting up again and discovered, to my amazement, that I was *pregnant!* 'Are you sure it's mine?' I shrieked.

What a shock! I had vaguely heard the ticking of a clock somewhere in the recesses of my brain but I was sure I had successfully convinced myself that it had nothing to do with my biology. Isn't it strange how a thought becomes a reality while you are still just thinking about it.

I drove home in a stupor and announced the news to my husband, John. He was thrilled but ever so slightly taken aback by my words, 'Well, *you'll* have to stay home and look after it!' Suffice it to say that after a somewhat troublesome pregnancy and an even more laborious birth, I was presented with the bundle of joy hereafter known as Sam.

Looking back on that hideous day in December 1987, I have to admit that I was not the only one who was traumatised beyond belief. Sam was in for the shock of his life. Before the agonising drama began, I had gone to great pains to do my hair and apply make-up for the big episode. For those who have been privy to this form of joyous event, you will know how ridiculous this was. I can't begin to tell you what I looked like after eight hours of labour, two epidurals and 'The Forceps Delivery from Hell' (or that's where it felt Sam was yanked from). It was really amazing that I ended up with such a placid baby, when you take into account the fight he had to get into the world and then being confronted with this bloated hag who looked old enough to be his grandmother.

However, we have gone from strength to strength, and I have discovered to my complete surprise that I really love being a mother—which is all well and good, but is it any reason to put myself through it again?

And this time I have no-one but myself to blame. This pregnancy was *planned*. How modern, how organised, how 'Oh my God, what have I done?'

They say that you forget the pain, but from the moment that my carefully collected urine sample turned clear in my doctor's office, the whole dreaded experience came flooding back. Now don't get me wrong, it is not the 'being a mother' part of it I hate—it's the nine-month lead-up to hearing the baby's first cry, that I could really do without.

With all the amazing advances in genetic engineering and birth technology, you would think that someone would have come up with a better *modus operandi*. The way I see it, that one brief shining moment of 'Yes, Colette, you are pregnant!' is fast overshadowed by nine months of constantly running to the toilet, insurmountable indigestion and heartburn, vigilant weight-watching and the ever-present sensation or—dare I say it—pain, of everything in your pelvic area feeling as though it is being stretched beyond all recognition.

This time has been slightly different for me, in that I began the second ordeal in a much healthier condition. However, I am still under the care of two doctors for the confinement, an obstetrician and a heart- and blood-pressure specialist. My time is divided between these two extraordinary men, and thankfully they have provided me with a great number of laughs. I hasten to add that I don't think they know for a minute how funny they really are.

The obstetrician has known me for a few years, but he still constantly surprises me. One vivid memory I have of him is, again on that fateful day in December 1987, when he arrived at the hospital to 'induce my labour'. He had just stepped out of the shower and with his slightly mad professor hairdo and the big rubber apron he had donned for the event, he picked up a giant crochet hook and came towards me.

'You look just like Sweeney Todd', I said.

'Who?' he said.

'You know, the musical about the mad barber, who cut people up and made them into pies?' I said.

'No,' he said. 'Now don't worry, this won't hurt a bit.'

Funny, I thought, that's just what Sweeney Todd said.

My favourite story of my other medico is a quite

recent one. At the beginning of every visit with this jokester I have to perform an interesting exercise called the 'mid-stream urine test'. If you have managed to get through pregnancy without ever being asked to do this, consider yourself a chosen child of the fertility gods. It is really hideous. I won't go into the physical mechanics of the act—it is enough to say that, as in a lot of other areas of obstetrics and its environs, this particular trick is not a very dignified one. On my last visit, I performed the act to the best of my ability, only to be informed by medicine's answer to Chevy Chase that I had failed my test. Too much miscellaneous product! I was devastated. Painful memories of failing Sixth Form Geography and the dressing-down I received from Sister Mary Una flooded back into my psyche. I was a mid-stream urine drop-out! Was there a supplementary exam I could take? Was there a course I could enrol in to improve my marks? All of these questions failed to raise even a smirk on Dr Chevy's face. This was a very serious business, and I should treat it as same.

'Did you face the toilet?' he inquired earnestly.

'No, I did not!' I replied indignantly. 'You may not have noticed, Doctor, but I don't believe that I am equipped for that sort of approach.'

Still no sign of even mild amusement. I decided to mark this one down to the medical profession and its general lack of humour. However, I have been practising my best mid-stream urine joke routines for my next visit.

One of my other whinges about the gestation period is the effect it has on my all-over appearance. In my pre-child bearing years, I am sure that I read somewhere about the fabulously fertile time it was in a woman's life. I saw pictures of women looking wonderful with shining skin, the no make-up look, and positively blooming from head to foot. Well, what happened to me? From the very moment those cells start to huddle into the embryonic cluster called life, all my nails immediately break off, leaving me with little butterstumps for fingers, my face begins to resemble a lump of dough with three holes punched in it, my hair falls out in clumps and when it finally does reappear, it grows back...grey!

Where is the expectant glamour here, I ask?

As I write, I am pleased to say that I am nearing the end of this, my *final* pregnancy—and so far so good. Compared to my first time 'in the pudding club', this venture has been remarkably normal. Apart from the enduring horror of the syndrome known as 'morning sickness', and the anxiety of the amniocentesis tests, my life as a human incubator has been almost bearable. Whoever it was that named the excruciating nausea experienced during the first trimester, 'morning sickness', was either totally misguided—or a man!

I've tried all the cures, and nothing works. I survived the odious period this time by watching daytime soap

operas and eating constantly. Thank God that, for me, this stage only lasted for six weeks; otherwise I would be the size of a house by now.

I only have a few weeks to go and I can really see the light at the end of the tunnel, so to speak. Last time I spent the final four weeks of the pregnancy in hospital... waiting. I am determined not to put myself or my family through that trauma again, because women in confinement, I am sad to say, become totally irrational, and I was a prime example of this.

Apart from the unaccountable bouts of moistness around the eyes, I once engaged in a battle to the death with the night nurse over a bunch of dead flowers. She was daring to remove them from the room!

Now I am eagerly awaiting the Next Big Day. I'm looking forward to the pain of first and second stage labour, and John has braced himself for another onslaught of the harridan-like language I assail him with during transitional labour. I learned all these fabulous technical terms at birth preparation classes last time. We decided not to attend again. No matter how hard someone pinches the fleshy part directly under the armpit as you breathe your way through the pain, it is my belief that nothing prepares you for that real feeling of pushing a watermelon through the eye of a petit-point needle.

One final thing I can be very grateful for is the fact that we wrote this book during the pregnancy and not after having the baby. I believe that it would have been near impossible to concentrate while sitting on a rubber ring, to ease that all too familiar feeling of having been perched on the Eiffel Tower and rotating!

3
Parenting—This century's greatest lie

From the very moment they place the slimy, slightly bluish little bundle onto your tummy, or whatever part of your anatomy you deem appropriate for the touch-down, the die is irrevocably cast.

Incidentally, have you ever wondered why the father is not stripped naked at delivery and the baby placed on his not-so-tender abdomen? But more of this later...

I have to say that apart from the overwhelming relief of 'Thank God that's over!' the other memory I have of *that* moment is the feeling of crushing responsibility.

I had been warned of this by everyone, from my concerned ageing aunties to Josie, the greengrocer's wife; from my 'You just wait and see' mother-in-law to my always caring but mostly vague husband, John.

But, as they say in the classics, 'You never really know until you're there'. (A very early Mona Mann classic.) When I was learning at the knee of the aforementioned philosopher, there was no real argument as to who did the rearing. In most cases, the mother was at home or in a part-time job, and she did all the day-to-day caring, peppered with the odd threat of 'You just wait till your father gets home'. After a certain age this menace became powerless in our house, because I had learnt to jangle my mother's nerves in such a way that she could never remember where to start when my father *did* get home.

Maybe that was the reason she was often heard to say, 'I only hope, my girl, that one day you have a child that's just like you!'

So where did it all change? When was 'mothering' transformed into 'Parenting'—and, more importantly, when did the dreaded Parenting become the biggest rip-off this century?

I don't want you to think that I have become a flag-waving, card-carrying, red, separatist, pinko man-hater, but I really think that in the whole scheme of things, we girls have been conned. I suspect it has something to do with the renewed education and interest in breast-feeding! I think this is where we let down our guard and allowed the ambush to happen.

One of the most enlightening times I have ever spent was the month I was incarcerated in the antenatal ward, waiting to give birth for the first time. As a special treat I was allowed to go for a walk—for five whole minutes—once a day. Oh, the decisions: when to go, where to walk, how to feel, what to wear?

Having coped with these momentous questions, I set off—to the nursery—to look over the latest batch of hatchlings. To my absolute dismay I found myself engulfed in a vale of tears. No! I wasn't crying (well, not that day, anyway), and the newborn babes were all snoozing happily. The wailing and gnashing of teeth was coming from the group of seemingly normal women sitting in a corner, clutching their offspring to their breasts.

'What's wrong?' I asked worriedly.

'It's my milk, there's not enough!' said one.

'She won't suck!' said another.

'They say that I'm not relaxed enough to let down [the milk]', said a third poor darling.

But 'Breast was Best' wasn't it? It all looked so natural in those magazines—I once saw a photo of one woman feeding twins at the same time.

'Just you wait and see!' warned the first mourner, 'you'll see how *natural* it is!'

Later the same day one of these girls popped in to see me in my 'cell' and I asked her why she was persisting with the breast if it really was not working. She said it was because her husband wanted her to breastfeed. 'Well, tell him to buy a nursing-bra and a breast-pump and come in here eight times a day and do it himself!' I said. She laughed nervously and said that most of the other women had the same problem and perhaps I should talk to them, too. I never saw her again.

I need to admit at this stage that I was one of the luckier ones who found the whole breastfeeding experience relatively easy. After you get over the extreme pain of chewed nipples, the odd bout of mastitis (a blocked and infected milk-duct), and have learned all the 'natural' methods of latching the baby on, knowing when he has had enough, building up your milk supply, regulating it (I think I could run a dairy farm now) and remembering to stay relaxed and calm at all times, there is nothing to it.

And the amazing thing about all of this is, it gives Dad so much more time in bed to rest up for his Parenting role.

Having survived this torrid time of being *the* life support system, you also have to suffer the regular humiliation of the weekly baby health centre visits. The much-feared weigh-in of the little darling was often closely followed by the words, 'Oh dear, not much of a gain this week. Now what has naughty Mum been doing?' I always had to fight an irresistible urge to scream, 'I've been out all night dancing with Sylvester Stallone in a disco. What do you think I've been doing?' Even on the odd occasion I was accompanied by John to these torture tests, I found it interesting that he was never put on the Parenting rack and questioned on Advanced Nutrition.

I must say that, as men go, John is better than most. He does attempt to help in whatever way that he can. However, discipline is definitely not his long suit. That age-old catchcry of my mother's would be plainly useless in our household. Both boys, my son and eight-year-old stepson, see their father as a total ally against me, the Commandant of Enemy Forces, and 'can't wait until their father gets home'. However, we both believe that children need limits in order to recognise the love we feel for them.

Being a first-time mother at the age of thirty-seven, I really felt that I needed to read up on the subject. During the first year of Sam's life, I must have studied just about everything written on child taming, and I can say that I gleaned only one really important fact: we don't bring up our children, they bring us up. It doesn't matter how much we read or are told about Parenting, the fact of the matter is children are just little adults waiting to grow up.

I once ventured into the wilds of a playgroup jungle, but I am afraid that it was too much for my non-competitive nature. I found that while the young cubs were playing and fighting over an astounding assortment of toddler trinkets, the big mama bears congregated into a huddle of colourful sweatsuits and headbands, and discussed such riveting topics as toilet-training (potty or the real thing), cloth or terry-towelling nappies, and the most curious of all—'And how many words does little Joshua have now?' I could never quite understand how any of these mothers had the time to sit down with a calculator and individually recognise, categorise and tabulate every gem of the English(?) language that dropped from their little ankle-biter's lips.

So Sam and I moved on from there, confident in the knowledge that he fully understood the inner meaning of the words 'big truck' and 'babby car'.

He now attends another class, an eighties' parenting phenomenon, called Gymbaroo. He likes this very much, because it means that after some 'silly' singing and dancing (his words, not mine), he gets to climb all over all sorts of equipment and pretend he is a monkey. And not one single person has inquired about his 'potty prowess'.

As you can see, I still have a long way to progress on the path to Parenting, but I am willing to learn. In fact, I can hardly wait till I am confronted with the question of the first Mixed Slumber Party. When I was growing up in the raging sixties with a widowed mother, the answer to these problems (when you dared ask them at the age of nineteen) was simple: 'No!' But I have a feeling, even with today's sexual attitudes undergoing an AIDS-related overhaul, this uncomplicated approach is long gone. I guess I'll just have to 'wait and see'.

My next and, indeed, more pressing hurdle to overcome, parentally speaking, is the birth of my next child. My co-author and close friend, Annie, is trumpeting quite loudly from her childless throne that 'This one could definitely tip the balance'. She wholly believes that domestic chaos is just around the corner for me. Much and all as I hope that she is wrong, I have a sneaking suspicion that there could be some truth to her words.

In a considered and intelligently nineties' approach to Parenting, we have been preparing Sam, who will then be two years and nine months, for the invasion of a new baby into the house. Following all the best kiddywink manuals, we have explained at his little blank face, all about the baby in Mummy's tummy. We have shown him pictures of himself as an infant, we have let him help us prepare the baby's room, we have even borrowed a friend's baby for Sam's closer inspection. No caring parental stone has been left unturned.

To test our progress in the acceptance of his new brother or sister, Sam's eight-year-old brother, Rhyss, one day asked him proudly, 'Where is Mum's baby?' Sam studied him for what seemed like ages and then finally said, pointing to himself, 'Sammy is Mum's baby!'

Rhyss rolled his eyes to the ceiling and said to me, the mother, 'Oh boy, are you in for a hard time!' And this Parenting pearl from the mouth of an eight-year-old!

TO BE CONTINUED...

4

'Mrs, Mrs, come quickly...'
A renovator's sentimental journey

With today's high cost of real estate, exorbitant mortgage interest rates and the particular trauma that comes with moving house, more and more people are choosing to renovate rather than purchase a new property.

For some arcane reason, we think that building an extension, whether up, out, or over the garage, will be much easier and more pleasurable. Proof positive, once again, that the world's gone mad!

One area of major growth in the building industry recently is the increasing number of single women who now own their own homes. And, like their married counterparts, they need builders, fix-it persons and a variety of renovations completed.

The first hurdle, and possibly the most difficult one, is to find a tradesman (sorry, but this seems to be the most common gender to turn up on the doorstep!) who will converse with you, the woman, as an equal.

It is truly a gifted builder who can discuss the work that needs to be done, sensibly and in a language we can all understand. So the first tradesman through the door who doesn't utter one 'Listen, lady!', with eyes rolling heavenward, or who doesn't express the slightest hint of a patronising sigh, should be given the contract.

After all, you will be practically living with this man for many weeks, more likely months, and possibly years, so a sarcastic wit is not what's needed when arguing over a broken bathroom tile at seven o'clock in the morning.

Running a close second to a good attitude is the significance of physical appearance. Smallness of shorts, tightness of buttock, stretch of singlet, size of bicep... are all important points for consideration. Having interviewed a seemingly endless array of applicants you might just be lucky enough to have Mel Gibson walk through your front door with a hammer! Admittedly this is a long shot, so a runner-up may have to be substituted.

This then establishes the option for an affair. However, before leaping into this arrangement, one should think about how it will affect the employer–employee relationship you now have with this person.

On the one hand, the idea of a brief fling with the burly hulk that stands before you, knee-deep in rubble, is quite appealing. On the other hand, you do want the renovation to be completed one day, don't you— and preferably before the year 2000?

It's a dilemma for the Nineties Woman!

Not that it's any easier when you're approaching the problem as a couple. No matter how intelligent, attractive or practical the woman is, your average Aussie builder not only will relate more successfully to the male partner, but will also find him and his life much more interesting. Don't try to fight this, just go with it.

Having established the ground rules of an appealing dress code and the pecking order of communication, it is now up to you, the owner, to learn the lingo of the bombsite you once called home. Learning to converse in the vernacular of carpenters, plumbers, plasterers, floor-sanders, tilers, electricians, damp-proofers, painters and bricklayers can be difficult at first, but in the long term well worth the effort.

If you think politicians have become the masters of saying one thing and meaning another, the definitive art of doublespeak must have originated in the building industry!

'No worries, she'll be right!' is the universal answer to everything, whether you're asking about the likelihood of striking rock during the initial excavation or the detail in the tail-feathers of the reproduction cassowaries to be mounted on the Doric columns leading to the jacuzzi.

Faced with this reply, you find yourself in a multiple choice situation as to what they *really* mean. Is it:

(a) Yes
(b) No
(c) Don't really know
(d) Who gives a rat's arse, lady?

The chances of (a) being the answer are pretty slim, (b) and (c) are always possibilities, but our experience shows the safe money is usually on (d). Don't expect too much—that way you won't be disappointed.

A friend of ours, foolishly, did expect too much. She assumed that her roofer's place of work would be on her roof, doing whatever it is that roofers do. Although confused by their actions, she never questioned what exactly they were doing *underneath* the house next-door. It wasn't until one day they staggered out of their makeshift den, climbed the ladder to her roof and promptly fell off, that she realised her employees must have been indulging in some extra-curricular artificial stimuli. There was an immediate shutdown on all work due to injury—and she vowed to show more interest in the future.

Another major area of conflict is the ever-present problem of 'supply'. For example, when your trusty building supervisor comes to you with the news that there will be a 'hold-up with the fire-place, owing to supply' what he's *really* saying is:

(a) He forgot to order the bricks.
(b) The bricks you chose are now no longer available.
(c) The bricklayer's great-aunt Bessie has come to stay.
(d) All of the above.

One more overworked excuse is the old stand-by about 'the plumber'. This particular cop-out, we suspect, is characteristic of the Australian species of bombsite overseer. Whether it be the laying of the kitchen floor tiles or the fitting of the Art Deco chandelier in the bedroom, the reason given for the delay of this work is always the same: 'Sorry, lady, we're waitin' on the plumber!'

Add to all these indignities the realisation that your

previously happy and well-ordered life has been reduced to dust and unimaginable degradation. Apart from picking the grit out of your teeth every morning in your long-suffering neighbour's bathroom, it's the frustration of having your life reduced to a paltry existence in a cupboard that has pushed even the meekest of violets over the edge.

Dyed-in-the-wool pacifists have been known to find themselves screaming like harpies and threatening physical violence of Rambo proportions. As strong as this inclination for savagery is, we petals of the gentler sex must try to temper our fury because such outbursts in front of our bombsite overseer do no good at all and go over his head like a hankie with the corners tied. After all, he has heard it all before.

Complain with dignity and style! Some suggestions to aid you when trying to achieve this:

(a) DO speak in your normal voice.
(b) DO use correct terminology.
(c) DON'T cry—they'll think you're pregnant, *AND*
(d) DON'T do it in your nightie!

The absolute depth of humiliation for the renovating consumer is to be sacked by your builder. Another friend of ours thought it not unreasonable to request the kitchen sink to be installed by Christmas. Silly her! He was going to Vanuatu for the holidays and the wife had already bought her leopard-skin bikini. Just when did she think he would have time to fit the sink? And, how dare she bother him with this nonsense on a Saturday night? He hung up in her ear and our friend never heard another word from him . . . not even a postcard from Vanuatu. Maybe she *was* asking too much, but, hey, who else was brave enough to take on an errant builder on a weekend?

Having shouldered the responsibility of 101 executive decisions each day and occasionally daring to feel quite pleased with yourself, you then have to contend with the added problem of your partner... Just when you think it's safe to fall into bed to gather your strength for another day, He's out there with a torch, demanding to know why the doorknobs are not on yet. 'Who gives a rat's arse?' you find yourself muttering under your breath... *And now He's threatening to do it Himself!*

As you lie there coldbloodedly plotting His murder before the concrete in the bathroom is laid, you console yourself by realising your approach to renovation using 'experts' is infinitely preferable to Him doing it Himself. The notion of doing it His way would score far too high a rating on the Spousage Stressometer to even consider discussing it at this time.

If you're about to embark on a renovation for the first time—Good Luck—everyone should experience it at least once. If you find yourself 'two bricks short of a load' and thinking of going through it a second time, re-read this chapter and, if that doesn't help, remember the rallying cry of the Renovating Addicts Anonymous Support Group: 'God help us... Never again!'

5

Mothers, fathers, ageing aunties, hippie sisters and partners' ex-partners

Solving the problem of the Sunday roast

It all starts so innocently!

You ring the doorbell and wait. Why are you here? You really could have done with another early night. This flu virus has knocked you about a bit. But Karen was insistent. 'Oh, come on, you've gotta come. I want you to meet this really "interesting" guy... No, it'll be nothing like that. It'll be fun—honest.'

Oh, yeah, great, you think to yourself. The door opens. You catch your breath. Now, *he* is fun. But with your luck, he'll be Karen's date.

You follow Him into the kitchen where Karen is whipping herself into a culinary frenzy. (Actually, she's having a little trouble with frothing the egg whites as it requires some concentration to do this while a man is blowing in your ear.)

You do a quick head-count and the realisation suddenly hits you. He who opened the door is the 'interesting' guy. You can't believe your luck! From that moment on, the two of you are welded at the hip.

You see each other the next day... and the next...

and the next. It's a crazy time. Your work suffers. All reason flies out the window. You're in love!

Then, one night, you hear the words that will change your life. 'I'd really like you to meet my family', He says.

Stand by. You are about to become a fully fledged member of Women Who Withstand the Weekly Roast with Relations.

And so begins your turn on the treadmill of you going to their place, them coming to yours, the occasional 'meal out' with 'the rellies', and, the most formidable feast on the family calendar, the merging of 'His people' with yours.

How many times have you crawled away from one of these family get-togethers and found yourself declaring to your partner, 'I now have a reason to save—to pay for a contract to be put out on your Uncle Joe!'

Apart from the ever-predictable arguments over politics, religion and the dire state of the trade union movement in Australia, the most exasperating aspect of these happenings is planning the menu.

His mother won't eat fish, your mother eats only fish. His brother, Bill, must have sliced white bread with every meal, while the new girlfriend, Tracy, drinks nothing but Advocaat and cherry brandy. Your hippie sister, Sandi, is a macrobiotic vegetarian and her de facto, Derek, won't eat after midday. Old Uncle Joe can eat only vegetables reduced to mush, and your niece, Kylie, fancies herself as an anorexic. And, as if that's not enough, His grandmother's second cousin, Drusilla, now acknowledged as the family national treasure due to her advanced years, exists entirely on a diet of marinated fillets of gilthead and eel pâté.

So that leaves you with a meal of... white bread spread with eel pâté, sandwiched together with mushy macrobiotic vegetables, on a bed of marinated fillets of gilthead, smothered in an Advocaat and cherry brandy sauce, and served to everybody but Kylie by 10 a.m.!

Now that the bill of fare is under control, all that's left for you to worry about is the mix of personalities.

One Christmas gathering at our house was made memorable by this blending of humanity. It was the first time that I had been awarded the honour of 'cooking the chook' for the whole family. My first husband's relations were a rather stilted bunch who saw themselves as impoverished gentry waiting out their time in the colonies. I felt they constantly hoped for a peerage to fall vacant so that they could make a triumphant return to the Old Dart in full chainmail with the Royal flag flying.

On the other hand, my mother, Mona Mann ('Mona by name and moaner by nature!'), who was 'dragged up' in suburban Brunswick, saw things very differently and knew when to call a spade a spade.

The occasion was progressing nicely; everyone was on their best behaviour. My mother-in-law even went so far as to say that everything looked 'quite lovely'.

I was bursting with pride. Then, the turkey was carved, the vegetables were served and the gravy was poured. Before settling down to revel in my gastronomic success, I grandly turned to my assembled guests and said, 'Now, is everybody happy, does anyone need anything?' To which my mother, in all innocence, replied loudly, 'I need stuffing!'

The words hung in the air. Needless to say, my in-laws never came for Christmas again!

6
Santa doesn't stop here any more

'Christmas comes but once a year...'—thank God! For an experience that occurs so seldom in our lives, why does the very word 'Christmas' fill us with such overwhelming feelings of dread?

When we were children, Christmas was a simple, uncluttered and, dare we say it, joyous event in our young lives. But with every passing year, as we battle our way to the next century, the whole yuletide business is becoming an endurance test of mammoth proportions.

The celebration has now turned into a mind-blowing chain of events from which there is no escape. Some of the more conspicuous of these seasonal skirmishes are: the ever-encroaching commercial lead-up to December 25, the panic of family festive organisation, the horror of Christmas shopping, the wrapping of gifts and the giving and receiving of same, the amassing of grocery supplies coupled with assembling the liquid refreshment, and, finally, the frenetic, all-suburbs crusade carried out in the family car on The Day.

In the past, the first signs of Christmas were never glimpsed before the end of November, at the very earliest. Today, the heralding of the silly season starts so prematurely we are lucky to survive April tinsel-free! With this rate of celebratory advancement, by the time we reach the year 2000, January 1 will have to be officially declared International Banning of 'Jingle Bells' Day.

As discussed in the previous chapter, the very mention of the words 'family' and 'food' can send shudders down the straightest of spines. However, add to this already volatile concoction the word 'Christmas', and you've got yourself one helluva set-to! Minor family differences, which at any other time of the year would pass almost unnoticed, develop into clashes of an order not seen since the Battle of Midway. The reason for this seems to be a combination of factors peculiar to this time of the year: the heat of the summer sun, the chemical reaction to Dad's homemade brew, and the all-important fact that if it weren't for Christmas this collection of people would never ever be seen in the same room together! We have a friend who has found this particular facet of the yuletide season so distressing that he once caught himself brooding about it in March.

A mandatory feature of The Great Christmas Campaign is the Battle of the Gift Gathering. This practice has got quite out of hand since its origins in the days of the dreaded Magi with their simple presents of gold, frankincense and myrrh. Today, the experience of Christmas shopping is a form of manual trench warfare. You are conscripted to enter the department store (hereinafter known as The Battlefield), where you find it necessary to dig in immediately—it's going to be a long day!

Everywhere you look there are queues of Gift Gatherers armed to the hilt, confusion abounds, and no orders from above are being passed down the line.

You discover to your dismay you are gaining no ground and are faced with the choice of hanging in there indefinitely or retreating from The Battlefield completely. The first alternative means you waste the entire day for the sake of three Christmas cards, a new angel for the tree and the joy of discovering that the Silky Mitt Depilatory Glove for Aunt Bessie is out of stock. The second option leaves you with an overwhelming feeling of helplessness and the glares of your teenage children as they say, 'Er, Mum, Christmas is looking a bit thin this year, isn't it?'

Accepting that you are Brigadier General in Charge of Gift Gathering, you are then faced with what to buy, for whom to buy, how much to pay when you buy, and where to go to do the buying. This isn't as easy as it sounds.

Entering the No Man's Land of Gift Giving is fraught with problems. There is always at least one Pesky Present Person who 'has everything' and is 'so hard to buy for'. The Precise Present Person is one who has made a specific request for something that you now discover is impossible to find.

And then there is the vast group of Duty Presentees —the people you 'have to buy for'. This mob can encompass anyone from the wife of your husband's boss to the office dork you managed to score in the grab-bag at work; or from your brand new mother-in-law who has never liked you anyway, to your second cousin's de facto's auntie because last year you turned up empty-handed and she gave you a 400-piece Royal Doulton dinner service. The strategy best employed for this contingent is to check your own drawers first, and if that doesn't prove fruitful, adopt a plan of incredible cheapness!

When receiving gifts from the other troops, try and keep a stiff upper lip and perhaps, if you can manage it, a hint of a smile. As one of our favourite American comedians, Henny Youngman, once said, 'I love Christmas. I receive a lot of wonderful presents I can't wait to exchange'.

Having achieved The Objective, the next major encounter is to get the damned things wrapped! This can be especially difficult if you have children who still believe in Santa Claus. There is nothing worse than sitting up late into the night frantically trying to wrap some unwieldy gift and finding it a new hiding place before dawn. And what about the trauma of running out of wrapping paper at 11 p.m. on Christmas Eve? What do you do? Wrap it in newspaper? A lasting memory is of us one particular Christmas Eve, long after the children had gone to bed, trying to build a sandpit in the pouring rain!

The Day arrives. It's hot. It's always hot.

You change your battle helmet and become Sergeant Major in Charge of the Officer's Mess. There're turkeys to stuff, hams to smoke, pork crackling to crisp and apples to sauce. And that's just before lunch! Of course, through all this preparation top priority must be given to the storage and refrigeration of the liquid refreshment for The Big Day. How often have you found your bowl of prized brandy sauce on the kitchen bench, curdling in the midday sun—but at least the beer's cold!

Having survived all this relatively unscathed for another year, there is one last push to make. Around mid-afternoon the rallying cry goes up: 'Everyone into the car'.

You start marshalling the kids, your husband's mother, her new boyfriend, his mother, and various other hangers-on, into the family vehicle because now it's time to go visiting. This particularly annoying custom, we believe, can also be blamed on the Magi. Just think, if those Three Wise Men had never seen that rotten Star in the East, and busied themselves by following it, we could *all* stay home on Christmas Day. As it is, we spend hours fighting the traffic in the heat of the day, only to go somewhere we don't want to go, eat food we don't need to eat, and smile bravely in the face of yet another useless gift.

'Christmas comes, but once a year is enough.'— Anon.

7

Weddings, parties... anything

How to behave at a function when you'd rather be somewhere else

'Do we really have to go?'
'Oh please, love. It's so important to me.'

How often over the years have we found ourselves trapped into this 'have to' situation. A function, officially labelled a wedding, a twenty-first birthday, an engagement, a christening, a funeral, a fiftieth wedding anniversary, or a dinner with the boss—this is the type of shindig we're talking about. These are gatherings to be endured rather than enjoyed. Whether you are attending as a partner, lover, good friend or 'handbag' (and we're not talking Oroton here!), there are certain 'dos' and 'don'ts' which are absolute requisites for complete survival in the world of inescapable get-togethers.

DO wear underwear in case you are required to dance on the table.
DON'T drink too much in case you are not required to dance on the table.

DO accept your partner's gift of a corsage graciously.
DON'T say, 'Where the hell am I supposed to pin this?'

DO smile sweetly at the boss.
DON'T stare at his wife's moustache.

DO congratulate the happy couple.
DON'T say, 'Gee, I really hope it lasts!'

DO dance with his drunken mates when asked.
DON'T make a fuss when they throw up on you.

DO eat the food.
DON'T wear it!

DO approach the buffet table hesitantly, serving yourself modest portions.
DON'T get panicky and jump the queue. (Remember to keep one hand free for cutlery!)

DO arrive on time for your best friend's wedding.
DON'T spend the night before with the groom.

DO offer your condolences at a funeral.
DON'T take photos.

DO choose your compliments to the bride carefully.
DON'T say, 'It's a pity you wore your hair like that. It usually looks so nice'.

DO take an appropriate gift to a fiftieth wedding anniversary.
DON'T present them with a gift voucher for a bungy-jump.

DO eat whatever is placed in front of you at the boss's dinner party.
DON'T dry-retch when you discover that the sweetbreads you are eating are really a sheep's pancreas.

DO try to enjoy yourself when participating at a christening.

DON'T shriek, 'You little bastard!' when the tiny tot chunders on your best shot-silk suit.

DO give your engagement gift confidently.
DON'T label it 'Return to Sender in Case of Break-up'.

DO spend a suitable amount of time at these functions.
DON'T ask to be taken home in time for 'The 7.30 Report'!

These are just a few suggestions to help weather the variety of beanfests one is forced to attend through the course of one's adult social life. Of course, there is always the chance that you could enjoy yourself. Admittedly, the odds are against it, but it is possible. Given enough warning before one of these outings, we have been known to whip ourselves into such a lather of dread that anything ends up being better than what we were expecting.

In the final wash-up, when all is said and done, it's really for the best that we go along as quietly as possible.

By adopting this conciliatory attitude towards weddings, parties... anything, we are then:

(a) strengthening the bonds of our partnership, or
(b) improving our relationship, or
(c) consolidating our friendship, or
(d) opening up a new career path, that of the professional 'handbag', or
(e) all of the above.

8

How to survive when your trolley of emotional baggage has a dicky wheel

Now that prime ministers have been seen weeping openly on national television for a variety of reasons, we can all feel free to air our emotions wherever and whenever we choose.

In the past, the subject of emotions and the displaying of same was always kept securely in the closet. Most of us would have some memory of an old auntie with a 'mystery' illness. 'It's her nerves,' they used to say in hushed tones.

The honesty of the 'let it all hang out' eighties brought us to our emotional knees. Standing firmly behind the opportune theory of 'go with the flow', we suddenly found husbands were confessing to extra-marital affairs, wives to extra tennis lessons, television evangelists to extra-curricular sins, and, most frankly of all, we found ourselves telling best friends that we never liked them anyway! And, didn't that make us feel warm and real?

One popular way of coming to terms with this volcanic limbo and sorting through one's compartments of emotional baggage was to enrol in as many self-improvement courses as were available. If you were successful in Hugging 101 or Second Semester Touching, your chances of a fulfilling life were greatly increased! Or at least that's what it said in the brochures.

An important ingredient peculiar to these personal awareness courses was the recurrent use of specific jargon. Friends you were once able to chat to quite easily, would suddenly emerge from 'a weekend of self-discovery' speaking in some obscure patois!

This was always rather unnerving.

You'd arrive home a little late one night, just in time to hear the closing theme of 'Neighbours'. Damn, wonder what happened? So, you decide to ring your best friend, Karen, to find out what went on in Ramsay Street that night...

'Hi, Kaz. It's me.'

'Oh, hi.'

'How was your weekend? Hey, listen, did you see "Neighbours" tonight? Can you believe I missed it? It was Jason's last night and everything!'

'No, I didn't watch it.'

'You're kidding? What were you doing?'

'I was dialling the Universe...'

'Ohhhhh.'

'The past weekend has changed my life. The old me was never in touch with her feelings. Now that I have worked through those primordial emotional layers and discovered my true self, I am making an affirmation. I will balance my biorhythms and re-focus the gelled edges of my self-image.'

'Oh... and I missed Kylie's final episode too. Bye.'

You hang up, feeling perplexed, hoping she was dialling the Universe toll-free.

So spins the carousel of emotional baggage into the nineties. Is it out of control? Where do our impassioned futures lie? What will be the latest craze? Skipping: The Path to Higher Self-Esteem? The Mystic Method of Energising Your Entrails? Or, perhaps, The Passion of Nose Exhaling: Save Your Marriage with One Blow?

With all these changes, one thing we can always count on is that old emotional mainstay—depression. Call it what you will—the blues, in the doldrums, down in the dumps, or exanimation(!?)—this feeling of despair has been with us a long time and is most likely here to stay.

The most important thing to remember when coping with depression is knowing when you are well and truly depressed. You must learn to grade the signs. For example, on a scale of one to ten, a small case of the 'blahs' would rarely get more than a three.

To be awarded the top score on the Scale of Low Spirits, one has to find oneself in a heap on the living-room floor, sobbing uncontrollably at the daytime soap operas. Oh God, they're starting to make sense to you!

Now is a good time to turn to the comfort of food.

At this stage, a big slice of bread, toasted, and dripping with butter and jam is the only answer. Maybe two, maybe three, oh what the heck, go for it—toast the loaf!

Another top scorer is when one is discovered home alone with every appliance and electrical device imaginable whirring, purring and *on*. The clothes being washed are on permanent spin, the coffee beans are ground to dust, the television is tuned to the SBS test pattern, and the CD is programmed on continuous cycle, playing Leonard Cohen's Greatest Hits.

Love your depression. Embrace it warmly. Make it your own, and then you'll know where you're coming from ... even if nobody else does!

Exploring and understanding your own personality can be a real eye-opener, especially to yourself. We knew this guy once who was 'exploring his inner self' and for 'homework' was required to do something that was totally opposite to his normal personality. He chose to wear a pair of bunny ears—honestly, a cute, fluffy pair with pink inserts! It was just something he felt he had to do. How much 'understanding' this provided him with is questionable but it certainly gave him a lot of sideways glances!

It's a personal choice and each of us may elect to do it differently. Bunny ears are not compulsory!

Confronting your fears and inhibitions can sometimes be the watershed in surviving the fast lane while riding the emotional trolley. A few years ago, filming a parachute course for a television assignment, we were interested to see that in a squad of twenty aspiring skydivers, there was only one other girl. She was slight, thin, really quite bird-like, and not the sort that you would expect to find in this macho bunch of daredevils. She seemed to be struggling during the twelve-hour training session, having problems with the landing practice and, indeed, the whole rigorous nature of the experience.

When asked why she had decided to jump out of an airplane at 2000 feet, she said, 'I've always been scared of heights and I thought this might help'.

We're not sure how much it did help, because she jumped all right, but on landing, she broke both legs. Now, she probably can't even get up on a kitchen chair!

9

Uh-oh, look who's parting his hair on the other side
The dead giveaways of male menopause

When we were growing up, the word 'menopause', if ever mentioned, was done so in a manner that was strictly hush-hush. Even though Mum was behaving quite irrationally, complaining of the heat in the middle of winter, and flinging off her cardigan continually, her condition was dismissed with, 'She's going through The Change'.

Simplistic as this explanation was, it is now a proven medical fact. Women in this particular age-group all go through this major hormonal adjustment.

So, what we want to know is, what's the boys' excuse for suddenly turning their mid-life crisis into *'male menopause'*?

To alert you to the onset of this trauma, you need to be able to recognise some of the early warning signs. Don't expect hot flushes. His ailment is a lot more subtle than that.

Our Dead-Giveaway List

1. When you realise the only attention he's paying you is to point out your faults.
2. When he asks you to start calling him by his full name, i.e. Ron becomes Ronald, Bernie becomes Bernard or Al becomes Aldolphous.
3. When you find he has taken to skin care in a big way.
4. When the tape deck in your car is jammed with his Guns 'n' Roses cassette.
5. When you find him reading his horoscope and planning his entire day around it.
6. When he buys a watch that tells the time in London and Khartoum and gives an hourly biorhythm readout.
7. When he wears your son's Pat Cash headband to the family barbecue.
8. When all he wants for his birthday is a pot of hair gel and a gym membership.
9. When you find his safari suit stuffed into the charity bag for collection by St Vincent de Paul.
10. When he starts to refer to himself as a 'dude' and addresses your best girlfriends as 'babe'.

This could be a lot for you to keep in your head, so you may like to copy this list and put it on your fridge under your favourite bumble bee magnet.

It should be pointed out that this is a list of early indications only, and if symptoms are allowed to persist the final outcome can be quite traumatic. Sadly, from our own observations, we have noticed that chronic sufferers of this syndrome more often than not find themselves alone, in a motel room, surrounded by empty pizza boxes.

A common manifestation of the disorder is the quick response to the faintest call of a young sex maiden.

Believing suddenly that he is on the downhill slope of life expectancy, he trudges to work, is flattered by the new nymphette on reception, fantasises himself into a frenzy, leaves his wife and kids for what transpires to be a momentary fling, is denied re-entry to the family home, and so ends his quest for his 'own space' in a pokey little motel room.

It seems to us to be the inevitability of accepting one's age that causes the problem in the male species. Little boys grow up to become bigger little boys who never want to be old men and, yet, we girls are constantly being told to grow old gracefully. So, come on, we'll let you use our hair gel, we'll join you at the gym, we'll even try calling you by your full name, but we draw the line at the heavy metal music!

10

You picked a fine time to leave me, you heel!

The agony and the ecstasy of divorce

If the word 'divorce' has no relevance in your life, past, present or future, then read no further. Turn the page and forget you ever saw it. But if you are part of that growing number of us who have experienced the trauma of a marital breach, you may find the following story of some comfort. I know that I feel better already just thinking about going public with the whole ugly mess.

Things really changed in the arena of marital disputes, with the introduction of the Family Law Act in 1976. Prior to this there was, particularly amongst women, a belief in the effort of 'staying together for the sake of the children'. Nowadays, I think it has definitely become a case of we women trying to get the men to take the children.

In my own case I'm happy to say that there were no offspring involved; well, not two-legged ones, anyway. Somewhere in the recesses of my mind I do remember a rather nasty altercation between my first husband and myself regarding the final custody of three likeable but incredibly stupid Dalmatians. I very proudly won that round, and assumed full guardianship of said animals—much to the chagrin of my present husband who has inherited the mantle of protection, without ever wanting it. It really was a case of 'Marry me, marry my dogs!'

Marital breakdown is insidious by its very nature. How many times have we heard a woman cry, 'Why am I the last to know?' Or indeed, as is often observed, 'The wife is always the first to know but the last to admit it'.

Either way, the Big D came as a huge surprise to me. There I was with the beef ragout in the oven, the table set for two, and he didn't come home. For two days! When the creep finally did turn up, I was furious. The casserole was ruined! Not that he was overly concerned. He arrived home, collected two pairs of underpants from the clean and nicely folded pile on the laundry bench and left, muttering something about needing some time alone to find himself. I guess he thought he wouldn't need socks.

So, there I was at the age of twenty-nine, in a completely gutted renovator's dream, and for the very first time in my life, I was alone. A sobering thought.

Drama of such epic proportions, I believe, can sometimes cause a squeezing of the brain-cells. In my case, in those early hours of that Tuesday morning so long ago, my feeble mind became fixed upon the gas hot water heater. You see, it had been in the house probably since it was built, some eighty years earlier. I exaggerate slightly, but this is highly emotional stuff we're dealing with here.

Anyway, my monomania with the old Rheem that October morning was that He had hatched some dastardly plan. He had always been the one to light the flare at the bottom of the antique appliance, because I 'would have blown us all up' if I had been in charge.

So, this was to be His strategy. He wanted me to do a Joan of Arc. Well, I'd show Him. A woman alone may be a lonely woman, but this little black duck had other plans. I went straight out that very day and ordered a brand spanking new, up-to-the-minute, water heater, using His bankcard. That got him!

One thing that I did learn from the entire melodrama of love, pain and the whole damn thing is that guilt plays a very important role and must never be underestimated. The feelings of blame, shame and 'All right, what's her name?' are something that grow and fester inside both parties, and therefore should be nurtured and used to great advantage.

If only we could bring ourselves to prey upon the emotions of others without delay. For example, when one partner decides to leave the other, the scenario usually unfolds thus: the departer is so riddled with guilt at what is happening and is so desperate to get out of that front door, with the two pairs of underpants, that they will say and promise *anything*, just to speed up the process. On the other hand, the departee is usually so surprised, shocked, nauseated and completely lacking in rational thought, that they do not have the presence of mind to take advantage of the situation, and get the weasel to put those reckless, guilt-ridden promises in writing.

The problem of the backlog in cases before the Family Court, and the overwhelming cost of same, would disappear if more people in this unfortunate situation could call upon their basest instincts, and stop trying to be so damned noble. As Norman Mailer said once: 'You don't know a woman till you've met her in court'.

In my own case, I know that I became a force to be reckoned with, legally speaking. But a woman scorned is a woman who quickly learns her way around a courtroom.

The division of property can be an absolute nightmare if not handled immediately. I forget how many times I contemplated ringing the police to report a break-in at the renovator's dream, only to discover that He had been around yet again on another reconnaissance and recovery mission. Learn from this—change those locks!

I must also confess that some years down the track, all this does seem funny to me, now. Anyway, bitterness can be so ageing!

Phew! Well, that feels heaps better now that I've got that off my chest! I hope it has been of some comfort to you, too.

# *H*ow to survive that abandoned feeling

Leave him first!

12

*Y*our best friend marries a dickhead—Handle it!

Call him what you will—a berk, a jerk, a dork, or a right git; a toad, a twerp, a smarm, or a sleazebag—nothing can improve the situation when your best friend marries one.

There you are having a fabulous day at home doing one of those wonderful 'girlie' things one does when one is alone—like cataloguing your shoes by colour—when the phone rings. You pick it up.

'Hi, it's me. You'll never guess, you'll never guess, you'll never guess! Go on ... guess! Give up? Give up??'

'Mmmmm.'

'I've met him!'

'Who?'

'Hiiiimmmmm! You know, the guy in Accounts Payable—the really gorgeous one—I've told you about him before.'

'Oh yeah, I remember.'

'He was in the milk bar across the road from work. It was amazing because he usually brings his lunch from home. I think his Mum makes it. Anyway, he must have left it on the bus or something, 'cause he was in the shop—he'd just bought a sausage roll. You know how I always have a sausage roll on Fridays—well, he'd got the last one. You'll never guess what happened next. Go on ... guess! Give up?'

'Mmmmm.'

'He said I could have his sausage roll! It was so fabulous.'

'Is that it?'

'Nooooo, silly. We walked back to work together and when we were on our own in the lift, he asked me out. So, last night we went to dinner. And, honestly, he's fantastic! He brought me flowers and everything. I can't wait for you two guys to meet. You're gonna love him.'

You hang up and return to cataloguing your shoes, feeling really pleased for your best friend. She hasn't been this happy in years. Now, if you could just decide whether to separate the boots from the shoes or go for a combined effect.

The weeks go by without further word, but this doesn't worry you. You know what it's like. The lovers would be out doing all the things that lovers do—going to the zoo on a weekday, hiring the video *Two Moon Junction* for a week at a time, learning to cook Thai food together, and buying expensive, new lingerie for her.

Suddenly, it's on. You have been summoned to meet Him. The vibe is still good. It looks like the real thing this time. The venue is her place and it's on for tonight. As you head off to dinner, you're sure it's going to be great.

'Come straight through, we're busy in the kitchen', she says.

(Ah, they must be cooking Thai food—so far so good.)

'Oh, you've brought wine. We're going Italian tonight, we'll use it in the pasta sauce', he says.

(Oh ... thanks a lot. It's always been good enough for us to *drink*.)

'Isn't he fabulous? I told you you were going to love him!' she says.

(Yeah, fabulous. I wonder if he makes his own pasta too.)

'We were just discussing superannuation. What scheme are you in?' he asks.

(The Snowy Mountains Scheme! What's it to you?)

The evening is all downhill from this point. Yes, he does make his own pasta (spinach and tomato). Yes, we do discuss superannuation all night. And no, they haven't hired *Two Moon Junction*. They have been watching *Wall Street*, and there is definitely no trace of lingerie.

As the dinner progresses, your best friend of fifteen years is fading faster than Grandma's chintz chair in the summer sun. Suddenly, the girl you have giggled with, gossiped endlessly with, and shared all your dreams with is gone. In her place is a stranger who discusses dividends and profit and loss sheets, can now understand Italian cookbooks without photographs and talks incessantly of restoring French Provincial armoires. How she can manage all this while gazing adoringly at a man wearing black leather pants and masses of chest jewellery is quite beyond you.

All the while that you are dealing with this transformation, he is all over her, billing and cooing like some demented dove on heat. As he is alternately nibbling on her ear and massaging her feet, he grandly baptises her 'Bouvala'. Just when you thought it can't get any worse, it does.

'We've decided to get married. As you can see, we've got so much in common. We were made for each other. Please be happy for us, we wanted you to be the first to know.'

(Oh, shit!)

He insists on walking you to your car, pointing out his new, mulberry Mazda RX7. He squeezes your hand in a show of camaraderie while giving you a mandatory peck on the cheek. 'I'm so glad we have finally met. Now I feel you're my best friend, too!'

(Oh, *shit*!)

As you pull away from the curb, watching him fade in your rear-vision mirror, you are overcome by a wet blanket of doom. Your best friend is marrying a dickhead.

On the drive home, you try to recall at what point in the evening you began to hear the siren of nerd-dom. Was it the sight of him drizzling King Island cream into his sauce di pasta macho, or was it the performance of cork-sniffing and wine-tasting afforded to *his* bottle of plonk while yours languished in the sauce? As you turn into your driveway, it suddenly hits you. Of course, it was when he began reciting to you at the dinner table the Desiderata in English, Italian and New Hebrew that the bells of sleaze really started ringing!

You can only hope it's a stage she is going through, but chances are you will be stuck with him for some time to come. Handle it. Maybe he'll be away a lot. Or, meet her for lunch during the week and, after all, there's always the 'girls only' night out.

13

It's in, it's out, it's happening, it's not

Fads for food, frills, fixes and fun

Much as we all like to think of ourselves as individual, original and 'doing our own thing', one way or another we inevitably discover that we are just part of the trend of the time.

This effort to be 'in with the in-crowd' engulfs all facets of our lives, whether we *want* to be 'in' or not. The latest craze of what we eat and where we eat it, what we wear and where we wear it, where we go and how we get there, and what the newest toys for fun are, bombards the senses through every waking minute of our day—and sometimes even when we're sleeping!

A personal 'fave rave' of ours, food, is in a permanent state of faddish flux. Generally speaking, during the fifties the tendency was to cook food until it was no longer recognisable. What was presented to you on the plate may have looked like lamb chops and three veg, but when you tucked into it, it all had the consistency of mashed potato. The choice for the three veg was also extremely limited—the first time a zucchini came into our house, all hell broke loose!

The sixties brought an exciting wave of experimentation. Flavour-enhancers came onto the market and became 'the greatest thing since sliced bread'. Suddenly the fifties mush had a taste to it! As inconceivable as it is to us now, a bestseller of the time and 'all the rage' was *Cooking with MSG*. (Don't try tracking down this gem of culinary publishing—we suspect it is now a collector's item!)

Having survived this chemical experiment, we then launched ourselves on a crash course to the absolute extreme—the health kick. The all-natural, grow-it-yourself-and-steam-it seventies turned our kitchens into something similar to a botanical nightmare. We had everything growing in them. There were the obligatory pots of parsley, sage, rosemary and thyme, layers and layers of planter trays sprouting alfalfa, mustard cress, and wheat grass, and, of course, no self-respecting health fanatic's kitchen was complete without the cultivation of the mung bean or the never-know-when-you-might-need-it terracotta pig full of elecampane root for *natural* antiseptic gargling.

Then came cuisine confusion. Whether it was *la grande cuisine, nouvelle cuisine,* or *cuisine minceur,* the sad fact was that there was never much of it! Presented as colourfully and innovatively as it was (who would have thought a Tiny Tim tomato could look, for all the world, like a peony rose in full bloom?), it never really stuck to the ribs. You always left the table wanting more—heaps more! The theory behind this style of cooking was to experience the taste sensation without consuming large quantities. The point was lost on many of us who had to stop on the way home for a hamburger—with the lot!

The last part of the eighties saw us reducing our red meat intake, downing copious amounts of mineral water, cutting back on salt, sugar and fats, while regularly rushing to the mobile unit in our local shopping mall for a cholesterol count. Time for another miracle cure—oat bran sales soared!

With all these munching modes behind us, we approach our food's future in the nineties somewhat hesitantly. Now when we whirl into our favourite Thai restaurant, we do have some residual nagging doubts. Are we about to eat enough roughage for our bowels, have the chemically cultivated vegetables been washed carefully, are the chickens free range, and, most virtuously, were the rice-pickers paid award rates?

Eating in the nineties is not going to be all beer and skittles!

But let's now give food fads the flick. What have we fancied in fashion? Here's our list. Remember these?

Twin-sets—nothing without a nice string of pearls.
Flares—a godsend for those with fat ankles.
Body-shirts—come on, guys, who were you kidding?
Platform-soled shoes—orthopaedic surgeons made a fortune.
Kaftans—uni-sex, but we all looked ridiculous.
Hippy headbands—long before Pat Cash.
Dirndl waists—had to be size 8 and six feet tall.
Nehru jackets—Kamahl still wears them.
Go-go boots—gone, gone.
False eye lashes—top lid, bottom lid, and that silly idea of sticking them on individually.
Mini—not a good look with fat knees.
Maxi—for standing still, too heavy to move in.
Midi—halfway between, didn't work either.

We can laugh now, but we all thought we looked fairly fabulous at the time. And, believe it or not, one day in the future we will probably find our favourite fashions of today pretty funny. Personally, we can't see anything amusing right now about shoulder pads, bicycle shorts, our penchant for 'power dressing', the use of colour consultants, the layered look or designer tracksuits, but who knows what will be 'funky', 'up to the minute', 'in vogue' or 'The Look' next year, or next month, or tomorrow? But whatever it is, we'll squeeze into it!

Fads come and go constantly in our lives. Some have come and gone so quickly we've missed them altogether. We're still feeling pretty miffed that Tammy Fay Bakker dolls never made it to Australia. However, we do have cupboards full of miscellaneous mania. We have nests of collapsible television tables, boxes of Splayds, two vertical grillers, fourteen very deflated beanbags, four strings of slightly worn love-beads, one framed Aubrey Beardsley print, three empty terrarium bottles, twenty-four litres of Mission Brown gloss paint, and a cherished mounted photograph of our canary yellow Mini Moke. Luckily, we still have our pet rock to use as a doorstop.

On the subject of pets, the live variety has not escaped the crazed clutches of the fashionable fad. In the seventies, the very latest in pooch-mania was the Afghan hound, a large dog requiring lots of space. For some extraordinary reason, the trendy owners lived by the rule that the smaller their house was, the more of this breed they kept. (The dogs always looked sad; perhaps this was why!) Peach-faced love-birds became all the rage until the owners noticed, to their horror, that these feathered friends' love for each other was short-lived, and, as they ripped each other to shreds, they were extremely noisy about it.

Other significant trends in the animal world were Abyssinian cats, Rhodesian ridgeback dogs (perfect if you needed a horse in your house), African ocelots, South American llamas, and the Alaskan husky. Thankfully for most of these animals, their care was so involved that the trend died out before the majority of them were yanked from their homelands.

The current direction in domestic pets is not so much the choice of animal but more what you can do for it and what you can buy for it to wear. You can take your pet to an animal psychologist, to discuss problems such as house soiling, chewing, unruliness, shyness, howling, and eating sundry objects. These days you can take your pet to an animal dietitian, an acupuncturist, an obedience trainer, a beautician or an animal gymnasium.

Fashions for our furry friends have not been ignored. Little tartan coats for terriers, dog booties, decorative collars studded with God knows what, ribbons and bows of every size and colour and for every occasion. Waterproof coats with lambswool lining are becoming all the rage and we hear the very latest is matching jumpers for you and your pet!

Other little humdingers available for the family menagerie are a cathedral cage for your canary, a house for your mouse complete with sky spinner and clip-on additions, and, if your bowwow is getting a bit rheumatic, you can treat it to a pet heating pad. It really is a dog's life!

Fun has not escaped the fingers of fad. Where we were once quite happy to surf at Bondi, waterski at Yarrawonga, and look down the blowhole at Kiama, today's thrillseeker demands to sample a little more of the world's exotica. Parasailing at Pattaya Beach, snorkelling at Monkey Mia, going down with the pearl divers at Broome or a peaceful trek through Tibet is far more the trend for this year's stylish tourist. Without a close relative in the travel industry, however, it is very hard to keep up with the latest destination. Heaven help us! You don't want to be caught at last year's resort in this year's climate!

Another area heavily influenced by fads is the issuing of names. Sadly for the bearers of some of these humdingers, their parents were caught up in a craze of some sort at the time of their birth and these poor things now must live with it. Moonglow probably won't sit well on a sixty-five-year-old woman, and it may be a bit of a shock today to have to call your plumber Elijah Blue.

So, if you want to be 'in' and happening, the path is clear. Be 'colour-assessed' before having lunch at your favourite Third World restaurant with your children, Sarah and Andrew. Arrange for your Abyssinian cat to board during your winter holiday in the Seychelles and book in for your final parasailing lesson before heading off.

NOTE TO READERS: Before acting on this advice, be sure to check latest trends. Keep in mind we wrote this chapter some months ago!!

14

Travel in the nineties—Exploding the myth

Travel is now part of our everyday lives. Fly to Perth for a meeting; school holidays in Fiji; dinner in Paris; or a wedding in Wagga—nothing to it! Any destination is possible. The glamour, the excitement, the exotic locations waiting to be discovered. But is it really the stuff that dreams are made of?

With the world's destinations becoming more accessible every year, it doesn't matter if you're married or single, young or old, man or woman, the opportunity to travel is there for the taking.

Once the decision to venture out has been made, nothing need stop you from throwing your proverbial wristwatch onto the highway of life and driving off towards the horizon—or flying away, which is more commonly the case these days. Your time is now your own.

Your head fills with romantic notions. This could be the adventure that turns your life around...thoughts of desert islands and millionaires' yachts, outstretched hands offering long, cool tumblers of colourful liquid, warm sands and blue lagoons, exotic destinations and Asian princes.

The day of travel finds you very quickly crashing down to earth again. Economy class is a great leveller—like death!

But, before any of this can become a reality you have to address yourself to the question of luggage. What quality and what quantity? Much and all as you've seen yourself in your fantasies with the Louis Vuitton luggage, separate hatboxes and matching make-up case, you'll soon realise this is totally impractical. For a start, how do you expect to be allowed this amount of baggage with an economy-class ticket? Secondly, a stopover in Bahrain could see an entire family moving into your hatbox, and, on top of everything else, you would have to contend with your make-up case being eyed off by some Qantas flight attendant!

So, don't go over the top, buy an average priced bag and take only what you can carry yourself. (No use kidding around, because the few porters that are available will be toting the Louis Vuitton of the people who are living out *your* fantasy!)

Packing your regular, run-of-the-mill bag is an acquired skill. The method Joan Crawford adopted of folding tissue paper between her dresses and into the sleeves, and stuffing it into shoes and handbags may seem a trifle excessive today. No amount of tissue paper would make much difference to a T-shirt, baggy track-suit pants and a pair of old runners!

So, now you're packed and ready to go. You prepare yourself to face that seething mass of humanity that is the airport check-in lounge.

Economy-class passengers cannot pre-book their seats, but you're always left wondering how all those people checked in before you. There must have been quite a queue at 3 a.m.!

No matter how early you arrive at the airport, it's

never early enough to secure a decent seat, if such a thing exists in economy class. All you want is a place by a window or the aisle but by the time you check in, it's not even a remote possibility. You're lucky not to be sitting on the wing!

So, you take what's left. A row in the high eighties with a seat marked by a letter sounding very much like it's in the middle.

You keep telling yourself that it won't be that bad. After all, what's twenty-eight hours sitting bolt upright, fully clothed, between one overweight passenger and another suffering from halitosis and verbal diarrhoea, experiencing interrupted sleep and consuming bizarrely packaged food?

There is always the chance you might sit beside someone fabulous and preferably of the opposite sex! But, sadly, most 'fabulous' people do not travel economy class. They are sitting snugly in their own Lear jets or happily ensconced in the pointy end of the jumbo.

Upon boarding the aircraft, economy-class passengers always make a sharp turn to the right. A left turn would find you in the luxury of first class and, tragically, that route is rarely an option.

You attempt to hold your head high as you start the long march to the tail of the aircraft. The worst-case scenario slowly becomes a reality. Your empty seat awaits you exactly in the middle of an already full row, with nary a Malaysian prince in sight.

You crawl over numerous pairs of legs into a space that seems much smaller than you remember it. You fasten your seatbelt to the sound of revving engines and the endurance test begins.

As you taxi down the runway a road tour in the trusty Commodore is looking better all the time.

Of course, in Australia you drive at your own peril. With many of the roads resembling the main streets of Third World townships, the chances of you and your vehicle reaching a destination totally unscathed are slim.

Hands up those who have been spared the all too common drama of a shattered windscreen. Well, aren't you the lucky ones? Obviously, when the semi-trailer zoomed past *you*, spraying rocks in its wake, you were parked by the side of the road changing a flat tyre.

And, if you do find yourself on a perfect, sealed stretch of road, forget about making up for lost time. There are police everywhere along the way with pens poised ready to issue your speeding vehicle with a ticket.

Of course, travelling with children either by aeroplane, car or camel train is a whole different ballgame. 'A joyous experience' is not one of the phrases that springs to mind when thinking of the various odysseys I have made in the company of my two children.

How many times do you find yourself saying, 'Now listen, [insert name], if you don't behave yourself, *you* won't be going anywhere, my friend'. At this point you always catch the offending child looking at you quizzically, as if to say, 'Oh really... and exactly how do you intend to leave me stranded here in this extraordinarily busy airport without finding yourself being exposed as a child-basher on Derryn Hinch's Blame File tonight... hm?'

A handy tip for keeping two or more young children together while travelling (short of tying them together with a rope) is to dress them in matching outfits. I admit that this is easier if they are of the same sex. However, either way, this theory never fails.

You see, because you are usually standing in queues for such a long time in public transport venues, if the children are dressed alike, they do attract attention, so that if one of the little darlings decides to make a bid for freedom, usually through some self-closing, steel doors to a quarantine area, you can bet that some obliging person will apply the bulldog tackle and bring the cute little runaway straight back to you. See, it really makes sense when you think about it.

In my short but chequered career as mother and stepmother, I have learnt that when travelling with the children, one should never expect too much. That way, it's easier on the nerves, somehow. Then, if by some fluke of nature, things do seem to flow with everyone having a pleasant time *and* all of us arriving at the same destination, we then have a good memory to spur us on for the next trip. However, it is only fair of me to say that these experiences have been few and far between.

My most hideous memory of travelling with the children was during the pilots' strike—whoops, I'm sorry, it was only a 'dispute', wasn't it?—of 1989. We had planned a family holiday at Noosa on Queensland's Sunshine Coast, two hours north of Brisbane... and we live in Melbourne. After much to-ing and fro-ing with some poor demented creature in the airline reservations office, it was finally ascertained that only *two* seats were available to Sydney, probably for the rest of time!

I grabbed those tickets with a firm grip, and decided that my husband could drive to Sydney and meet me and the children the next day. From there we would all pile into the family Camira and drive the rest of the long journey to Noosa, with an overnight stop on the way. Without going into the incredibly ugly details of the car trip, suffice it to say that the pilots' dispute would have been over in a jiffy had our Prime Minister and the President of the Australian Federation of Air Pilots been made to spend one hour in a Camira with my children!

15

A salute to cellulite—Phasing fat into fit

'Gym—I'd rather be eating cake!'

Have you ever found yourself lying on the broadloom of some gym, legs akimbo, kicking aimlessly, to the strains of Marcia Hines's version of 'Something's Missing in My Life' and wondered what the hell you were doing there?

According to the Macquarie Dictionary, cellulite is defined as: 'fatty deposits, resulting in a dimply appearance of the skin, which *cannot* be removed by dieting or exercise'.

So, what's the point? What has been driving us 'porkies' in the Western World to dream the impossible dream? To fight the unbeatable dough? To ride when our thighs are too weary? To jog where the stout dare not go?

Because all we want to do is to tuck a shirt *into* our jeans! Just once. Is that asking too much?

Yeah, yeah, okay, we want to be fit and healthy too. S'pose.

From a very early age we become familiar with the idiom of podge. Phrases like 'puppy fat', 'big for her age', 'she's a good eater, isn't she?', 'well padded', 'not fat—just chubby', and, our favourite one, 'at least she's healthy!' became part of our everyday life. No matter how it was expressed, the truth was there was far too much of us to squish into the elusive size 10 we craved.

And so started the unending cycle of lettuce leaves, black coffee, cottage cheese and Ryvitas. We all have our own, individual motives for putting ourselves through this torture, but some of our classic ones are:

1 When your back gets fat.
2 When your miniskirt is wider than it is long.
3 When all you yearn for is some chin definition.
4 When the tradesman asks which month the baby is due!

What to do? Which diet? What to eat? The Grapefruit Diet? No, citrus fruits give me a rash. The Israeli Army Diet? No, I knew a girl once who chose Port Salut for her 'cheese day' and you couldn't get near her for weeks. The Mayo Clinic Diet? No, eggs can be so hard to boil. The Beverly Hills Diet? No, where will I buy persimmons at this time of the year? The Pritikin Diet? No, I'm not that desperate yet! The Hip and Thigh Diet? No, my problem is bigger than that. Or, I know, The Scarsdale Diet? No, he was shot dead by his lover, wasn't he? I bet she was on Day Three of the Diet!!

Apparently, the answer is to eat sensibly, but who wants to eat lentil lasagne and low kilojoule French dressing for the rest of their lives? Not us, that's for sure. There must be another way.

Exercise! Win the war against weight with a workout! The history of physical jerks has been a varied and curious one. Every couple of years or so, a new-fangled fitness fad emerges as the saviour to all our bodily woes—and usually with a new outfit to go with it!

Jogging always poses a problem—it is so hard to endure the pain of bruised eyes and knees while the search for the perfect sports bra continues. Aerobics, whether we're talking low-impact, new body, or otherwise, is a definite no-no, because if you are not already thin, heart failure can be bad for the gym's business! Jane Fonda's workout video presents a real dilemma. How can you be 'going for the burn' with Jane if your television is tuned to 'Another World' and detailing the 'Days of Our Lives'?

Power walking has become fashionable recently, but we have noticed one hitch. It's best executed under the cover of darkness because, frankly, it makes you look quite absurd. Working out with weights is a big benefit if body sculpturing is what you are into. Unfortunately, you might be deterred by the names of some of the equipment, like lateral pull-down, hip flexer, and the abdominal crunch. And, when you come to think about it, why learn to lift a fifty-pound weight when you're not allowed to carry that much on a plane!

This leaves us with passive exercise equipment, where supposedly no effort is required to decrease fat or increase fitness. As much as this appeals enormously to us, unfortunately it is considered of little value. The followers of this system tend to use the tape measure to record results, rather than the weight scales. The method seems to move the fat around so that, thrilled as you are to lose two inches from your waist, you look down to discover they're on your knees!

So, sadly, tedious as it seems, the answer is the combination of the two: eating sensibly and finding an exercise programme that suits you. Look, we're sorry. We have tried to disprove the overwhelming body of evidence that is mounting against us 'porkies' but we have to concede defeat. However, there is a glimmer of hope on the roly-poly horizon. The personal fitness trainer. (For standard of applicant, see builder's qualifications in Chapter 4, page 21, and delete 'the hammer'.)

We've recently discovered the joys of having a personal fitness trainer. Apart from having someone who can actually find your pulse while you are huffing and puffing and going very red in the cheeks, they keep you honest. They are able to count better than you, they are deaf to your cries of agony, and they've learned to smile in the face of your abuse.

One more suggestion is to drag a friend along. The competition does wonders for your diastolic blood pressure! And it gives you someone to have a cup of coffee and a cake with afterwards!!

An Eye Fitness News Update!

A report just to hand has flashed across our Nubile News Desk. The latest crazes for the achievement of a beautiful body and a healthy heart are two new phenomena, direct from the US of A: step-up aerobics and cardio-funk. For the moment, this is all the information we have but as soon as we have figured out the right outfits to wear, we'll be there!

16

The voting game
Who wins: them or us?

[*Cue the theme music*]
Announcer: Good evening, ladies and gentlemen, and welcome to 'The Voting Game', Australia's most popular contest. Yes, folks, it's election time again. No, I'm not your host for this evening, I'm the warm-up man. My name is Little Johnny Howard.
[*Cue applause sign*]
[*Silence*]
Announcer: Now, come on, everyone, fair's fair, you've got to clap at least once. You know you've been specially selected for tonight's show. You've been bussed in from the marginal electorate of Swinging Voter Hills and you are very important to us. We're only doing this for you. So, let's go. One, two, three—*clap!*
[*Cue applause sign, again*]
[*Silence, again*]
Announcer: Oh, well, don't worry, we'll have another practice in the commercial break. Okay, we're starting now. This is live!
[*Cue the theme music*]

Announcer: Good evening, ladies and gentlemen, and welcome to 'The Voting Game', Australia's most popular contest. Yes, folks, it's election time again. Could you please put your hands together for the star of tonight's show, and your host for this evening, Senator John Bu-u-u-tton. *[echo effect]*
*[Cue sliding doors on host set. Senator Button jumps out, hopping and dancing wildly, clicking his fingers and appearing very animated. (*Note: *Senator could perhaps attempt a knee-slide here.)]*
[Cue applause sign]
Announcer: [Aside] Sorry, Senator, we know the clapping's not good. We're still working on it!
Host: Hi-de-hi, everybody. Button's the name; hosting's the game! What a show we have for you tonight. And, aren't you a bright-looking audience? I've always recognised the intelligence of the Australian electorate, too. And, someone else that I recognise is my beautiful hostess, Janine Haines. Come on, Ninny!
*[Cue those sliding doors, again. Janine Haines jumps out, hopping and dancing wildly, clicking her fingers and appearing very animated. (*Note: *Ninny should not attempt knee-slide here.)]*
Hostess: Hello, everybody. Good evening, Senator. And, a very good evening to all of you at home.
Host: My goodness, Ninny, this is some outfit you've got on tonight. Can you tell us a little bit about it?
Hostess: Why, certainly, Senator. It is made of hessian material, which, as you know, is a natural fibre, and as well, this particular garment has been recycled. It started life as a potato sack but I have this little woman who sews for me and she reworked the logo on the front into an old Aboriginal motto.
Host: Oh really, Ninny. And what does it say?
Hostess: 'Get Your Mitts Off Our Land!'
Host: And who are our contestants for tonight, Ninny?
Hostess: Well, Senator, tonight our carry-over champs

are, of course, the Labor Party. Their representatives are Bob Hawke, who's a Prime Minister from Canberra and says his favourite hobby is to be photographed with winners—of anything—and Paul Keating, who likes to be known as the World's Greatest Treasurer, is also from Canberra and has a number of interests which include Italian suits, antique clocks and commuting to Sydney.
[Cue applause sign]
Announcer: *[Huffily]* Oh, so now you decide to clap!
Host: And our challengers for tonight, Ninny?
Hostess: Well, Senator, I believe it's to be the Coalition but there seems to be a problem with sorting out their representatives. *[Turns to camera]* As you know, viewers, the game only allows three players per side and the Liberal-National challengers have turned up with a mob of sixteen! We understand that a final decision is imminent as to who will be representing them tonight.
Host: Well, thanks, Ninny. And now, it's time for a word from our fundraisers.
[Cue applause sign and theme music into commercial break]
Announcer: Okay, okay, audience, the applause for the Labor contestants was good, but remember, there has to be equal clapping time for the challengers. All right, all right—we're back. This is live!
[Cue theme music]
Host: Hi-de-hi again. Our challengers have finally arrived at an amicable agreement, and, Ninny, I think you've got the names there?
Hostess: Yes, Senator, I have. Their representatives are John Hewson, a doctor from Sydney, who lists his hobbies as sports cars, marriage and taking on seemingly insurmountable tasks, and Andrew Peacock, a former Opposition Leader whose interests include bronzing and marriage—and, believe it or not, Senator, this is Andrew's seventh time as a challenger on the show.

Host: What a survivor!
Hostess: Our third and final challenger for tonight is something of a surprise. He is John Elliott, a beer baron from Melbourne whose pastimes are a real mixed bag. He enjoys making jam, marriage and upsetting everybody.
Host: You carry-over champs are still happy with just the two of you playing for your side?
Paul Keating: Yes, Senator, you old scumbag, we are.
Bob Hawke: Arrghh ... yes.
Host: Well, okay. Because you have chosen to waive your right to a third player, our executive producers, Bill Hayden and his lovely wife, Dallas, have decided in their wisdom to take up their option and they have named an Independent substitute, Ted Mack, to represent The People.
Bob Hawke/Paul Keating/John Hewson/Andrew Peacock/John Elliott and Little Johnny Howard: Wнннннаааатт!
Host: Sorry, gentlemen, it's the Westminster system of government. The decision is final. Can we now please get on with the game? Round One. See you in the Prize Shop, Ninny.
Hostess: Good luck, fellas. You're on your own now.
Host: 'The Voting Game' has surveyed six million Australians and come up with the top answer to this question: 'As we move into the nineties, what issues concern Australians most?'
Bob/Paul: Buzz!
Host: The Labor Party, your answer, please?
[Bob and Paul go into a huddle.]
Bob: Arrghh ... Paul and I have discussed this at length and, considering the intelligence of the Australian electorate, we believe that what concerns them most is the colour combination of the uniforms in the one-day cricket series.
Host: No, sorry, you seem to have lost touch with The People on that one. We will have to go over to the challengers.

[John, Andrew and Mr Elliott are wrestling with their answer. John pulls himself free.]
John: We've come to expect that sort of inane response from the Labor Party. It's a mystery to us how they have been the champs for so many years. It's so long since they've had to worry about the needs of the Common Man that they've forgotten what they are. It's the workers of this country who have...
Host: Could we just have your answer, please?
John: We are finely tuned to the worries of the Australian community at large. We know the hardships people are facing today. We feel for every one of these poor wretches and we are attempting to address the problem. We...
Host: Quickly, challengers, please.
John: A Mercedes in every driveway!
Host: Sorry, no. I guess the Coalition hasn't quite got a grip on the balance of payments. That leaves us with The People's representative—Ted, your answer?
Ted Mack: Well, Senator, it is my belief that what concerns the Australian people most is the state of our economy, the protection of our environment, and a future for our children.
Host: Yes, you're absolutely right.
Bob Hawke/Paul Keating/John Hewson/Andrew Peacock/John Elliott and Little Johnny Howard: Whhhaaatt!
Host: Order! Order! Gentlemen, please. Now, Ted, it's time for us to go shopping. Ninny, what have you got in the Prize Shop?
Hostess: Well, Senator, it's going to be a difficult choice tonight. We have a beautiful leather-bound copy of a book written by one of our ex-challengers entitled 'Don't You Worry About That!', fourteen packets of recycled typing paper for the environmentally conscious office, or a brand new 300SE Mercedes Benz complete with a complimentary diamond-studded key ring.
Host: Thanks, Ninny. Quite a choice tonight! So, Ted,

what will it be? You've got twenty seconds.
[Cue think music]
Ted Mack: I'll take the recycled typing paper, thanks, Senator.
Bob Hawke/Paul Keating/John Hewson/Andrew Peacock/John Elliott and Little Johnny Howard: Whhhhaaaatt!
Host: Wow, what a game! Stay tuned, we'll be back after this word from the Speaker of the House.
[Cue applause sign and theme music into commercial break]
Announcer: Yes, yes, wow, what a game! In all my years in 'The Voting Game', I've never heard a winner answer like that one. All right, all right, audience, we're back. This is live!
[Cue theme music]
Host: Hi-de-hi again. Well, time's run out on us tonight, but the game's not over yet. As we all know only too well, this is just the beginning of a very big campaign and a night can be a long time in 'The Voting Game'! So it's goodnight from our carry-over champs...
Bob: Arrghh... goodnight, voters.
Paul: See ya, scumbags.
Host: And, it's goodnight from our challengers. Can we expect the same team tomorrow night?
John: Yes, Senator.
Andrew: The reality is... Absolutely.
Mr Elliott: I wanna see you boys outside! Goodnight, Australia.
Host: And, goodnight to tonight's winner...
Ted Mack: Cheerio, viewers.
Host: Last but not least, a big goodnight to my team: my announcer, Little Johnny Howard and, of course, the lovely Ninny, Janine Haines.
Hostess: Goodnight, Senator. Goodnight, Kingston!
[Cue applause sign and theme music into final credits]
Announcer: Okay, okay, audience, it's all over. Oh, very funny—there's no point in clapping now! Who needs you? We've got the single-issue groups coming in

tomorrow night! Start moving into those buses.
Hostess: Pssst, Johnny. Got time for a quick drink in my dressing-room?
Announcer: [Sighs] Sorry, Ninny. I'm rostered on to drive the bus tonight.
[The studio is in darkness]

The Voting Game. Who wins—them or us?

*C*auses for the nineties— A list, but it's ours

Something that characterises us as human beings is our ability to embrace a good cause when the mood strikes us. And, boy, have we been in the mood to embrace causes this century! From the struggle of the suffragettes to the fight for clean air, we have distinguished ourselves in our campaigns, demonstrations, street marches and rallies. Far be it from us to decry or dismiss any of these past crusades, but with the year 2000 fast approaching, we felt the need to evaluate what really bugs *us* now. To guard against the horror of one day finding ourselves at a loose end—as rebels without a cause—we have prepared a list ahead of time.

1 *E*nvironmentally safe sex— Don't abuse it: re-use it

THE SEARCH FOR THE RECYCLABLE CONDOM CONTINUES

In our extensive research into the subject of Sex and

Our Environment, we have discovered a whole problem area that has been ignored by science and technology: how to dispose of all those *rubber* condoms.

Just take a moment to think about it!

What's needed here is investigation into an environmentally safe and ecologically sound form of the old French letter. Our suggestions are:

- (a) Condoms made from recycled paper—messages could be written on these for sexual communication exercises.
- (b) Edible condoms—made from sausage casings and in a variety of flavours—great for barbecues. We've had edible panties for years, so why not condoms?

2 *The Love It, Eat It and Lose It Diet—Lose Six Kilos a Day without Leaving the Table*

This may sound inconceivable but if a three-year-old Neil Armstrong had been asked if he wanted to be the Man in the Moon . . . well, the rest, as they say, is history! For years we have subjected ourselves to a diet of eggs, grapefruit, Israeli cheese and lean meat. The time is now here for us to have it all. At regular intervals, the food scientists regale us with a new and amazing food fact. What better cause could there be than to get these boffins organised into researching a diet that is not based on our bodies' *needs* but on what these little bodies *want*?

3 *Save the Spur-winged and Masked Plovers —Not So Much Endangered Species as Really Well-dressed Ones*

Every self-respecting crusader has to have at least one

animal rights cause in their bag of worthy tricks. Mankind may have misplaced the dodo, but it does continue to make in-roads into the protection of everything else that moves, from the African elephant to sperm whales; from cute little baby seals to the recently much sought-after scrotums of kangaroos. So as not to leave *our* list incomplete in this popular compassionate area, we have searched the world for a suitable object of our charitable endeavours—whether the poor little Masked Plover wants it or not. (And who could resist this miniature Zorro of the bird world? He looks so cute in his enclosure at the Melbourne Zoo.)

4 *The Fighting Fund for the Humping of the Hills Hoist Back into Its Natural Habitat*

For a long time now, this homegrown contraption of wire and steel has been much maligned. The joke has gone far enough!

Beware, the resurgence of the Hills hoist is coming. Consider all the benefits you may have missed out on, just for the sake of a brick-paved terrace courtyard or a clear stretch of lawn:

- (a) Low power bills—it costs nothing to dry your washing in the open air and it saves energy, too.
- (b) Fresh-smelling clothes—without the use of those 'dryer sheets' which smell like a recently cleaned public toilet.
- (c) Built-in party decoration—there is nothing more satisfying than a gaily decorated Hills hoist for all your outdoor functions. Fairy lights, ribbons, and the odd star or angel for that very special Christmas occasion, will add a sparkle to any gathering.

(d) Endless enjoyment—how many people have deprived their children of the extraordinary pleasure of running through corridors of sheets and towels hanging on the washing-line?

When was the last time the little darlings asked to watch the clothes dryer being turned on? You've deprived yourself too—go on, run outside into the sheets and remember how good it feels. And, best of all, this is Aussie-made enjoyment!

5 NAGGA (National Advisory Group on the Glossamia aprion)—
A Research Project into the Mouth Almighty

The *Glossamia aprion* or Mouth Almighty is a fish found in the tropical waters of northern Australia. It is carnivorous and is usually found on its own. 'What's so special about that?' you think. Well, it has the amazing characteristic that the male of the species broods the eggs in his mouth until they hatch. We find this absolutely fascinating and, with the current advances in genetic engineering, we can't see why this talent of the Mouth Almighty cannot be researched thoroughly, and immediately adapted to the human male. We realise there could be some minor physical problems to be dealt with here, such as the size of the human male's mouth, his digestive system, and so on, but we feel confident that a bit of streamlining and customising should take care of any such hiccups. The women of the world will wait with baited (sorry!) breath for this one.

6 Act-Aid—A benevolent Society Formed to Raise Money to Finance Acting Lessons for Ridge Forrester

He's bold, he's beautiful—but if only he could act! We've followed young Ridge's movements through soap since he first burst onto our daytime screens some three years ago. Admittedly, his life in the Forrester mansion has not been a bed of roses, but how stoic can one performance be? The boy has got to learn to unclench that jaw! C'mon, Ridge, we're all here for you. We feel sure that with the support of Act-Aid you will give old Hollywood a real run for its money. Forget Tom Cruise; the sequel to *Born on the Fourth of July* will be yours. (Any reader who dares to doubt the validity of this cause need only tune in to 'The Bold And The Beautiful' each weekday.)

Well that should keep us busy for the next ten years!!

18

You oughta be congratulated. They said you'd never make it...

Advertising—Oh, what a feeling!

> Oh, what a feeling, a night of TV,
> What's your reaction when the ads come on?
> Yes, no, perhaps a cup of tea,
> Walk out, have a wee, put the kettle on?
> C. MANN AND A. PAGE

Where would we be without advertising? Just like National Nine News—Imagine Life Without It. We wouldn't know A Great Way To Fly; or Where's The Cheese; or Which Bank; or who to congratulate for the tub of margarine.

We would sleepwalk our way through our bland existences and never once experience the exhilaration of Letting Our Fingers Do the Walking. How could we possibly contemplate a life without Footballs, Meat Pies, Kangaroos and Holden Cars? Like it? We'd hate it!

Advertising, whether on television, radio, billboards, or in the print media, has become an intrinsic part of our everyday lives. Without even realising it, each and every one of us is some sort of target for some hot-shot, creative whiz-kid conceptualising in some state-of-the-art advertising agency somewhere in the world.

So, we're in safe hands! See how we're being looked after? You can appreciate how much in common these so-called visionaries of our lifestyles have with the majority of us. Sitting in their pale pink offices, enthroned in their ergonomic chairs, or meditating on their Persian dhurrie rugs, they are completely in touch with the needs of the average, Australian family in the suburbs.

No aspect of life escapes the far-reaching tentacles of advertising. Everything and everyone becomes a commodity. Something to sell to somebody. We have had campaigns to market everything from pet food to paint, from cars to Coke, from beer to banks, and from politicians to presenters of news.

Now the dog knows that Your Best Friend Deserves Good-O and you know you sure can Trust British Paints. You can feel safe that the little car salesman will Do It Right For You and Things really do Go Better With Coke. They Said You'd Never Make It but hopefully you did, even though the Bank Never Forgot It Was Your Money. And, now It's Time To Turn On The Lights but only because Brian Told Me, Brian Told Me, Brian Told Me So!

But let's not condemn these gurus of the commercial too quickly. Life in Advertland can be real tough for the Creative Director. He or she is only as good as his or her last campaign. Some products will sell themselves while others can be a real headache for these Crown Princes or Princesses of 'The Plug'.

A glamorous product, such as Coca-Cola, has had the same basic format for its advertising for decades. Apart from finding a new bunch of young bodies and yet another exotic beach location, the advertising agency's professionals have a fairly easy time of it. But just imagine how one of these vital, young vision-makers would cope with a $10 million national campaign to promote the use of Chicken Manure.

From the outset, a number of decisions need to be made. How do they want to push this Chicken Manure? Do they go for the hard-sell and hit the audience with an arrogant little salesman who shouts threats at them to buy it or else? Or, is soft-sell the way to go, wooing the viewer gently with the homespun story of every-day life with a subtle mention of the product name at the end? Or maybe an anti-ad, with visual images of everything but the product being advertised and leaving the consumers totally confused as to what they are supposed to consume?

Considering the account is worth $10 million, any admen worth their salt would see the benefit of submitting proposals for all three versions...

Australian Chicken Manure—Proposal No. 1

WHERE D'YA GET IT? LOOKS GOOD, FEELS GOOD, IS GOOD!

Open on salesman dressed in a dark, conservative suit, surrounded by bags and bags and bags of the product. The scene could be strengthened by the use of some chicken feathers and a few eggs. The salesman (preferably a Lou Richards or Rex Mossop type) starts his spiel.

'Has your lily gone silly; is your rose on the nose; is your plum looking dumb; or has your apple got the dapple? If you can answer yes, yes, yes, yes *[use of echo effect would be helpful here]* to this question, you need Aussie Chicken Manure. "Where d'ya get it?" I hear you cry. Well, I'm just the man to tell you. We are full of it and we want to offer it to you!'

While the talent is delivering his dialogue, we anticipate rolling graphics from the bottom to the top of the screen, listing the outlets where the product will be available. The faster these graphics speed past, the better. We are going for a real sense of urgency here!

'You can spread it, you can rake it, you can dig it in, or you can just throw it around—Aussie Chicken Manure is the dung for you. Your vegies will thrive, your fruit will flourish, your trees will blossom and your grass will grow with Aussie Chicken Manure.'

At this point, a person in a giant chicken suit will scratch their way onto the set, pecking at the bags of manure. The bird strips one open and, with its claws, spreads it over the floor area. Having done this, the bird then lies down to wallow in the stuff.

'Now, listen up, all you gardeners out there. I'm only gonna say this one more time—Aussie Chicken Manure —it's the toppings in droppings. Did ya hear me? Aussie Chicken Manure! You'll be kicking yourself if you miss this one. This is positively the last time it will be offered at these low, low prices. *[Insert graphic with low, low price here.]* And, as me old mate here *[gestures to the person in chicken suit]*, Chicka the Chook, says...

Person in chicken suit jumps to its feet shouting, 'Aussie Chicken Manure—looks good, feels good, is good!'

Then, talent and chicken squawk together, 'Aussie Chicken Manure!'

*A*ustralian Chicken Manure—Proposal No. 2
YOU, YOU MAKE ME FEEL BRAND-NEW

The setting is Grandma's place, an exquisitely laid-out English-style cottage garden. Grandma, a beautifully groomed, grey-haired woman (in the style of the Queen Mum—check her availability) is tending her flower-beds, while her extremely attractive and immaculately dressed grandchildren frolic playfully with the golden cocker spaniel nearby.

The look should be soft, nostalgic—well, slightly out of focus, anyway. It's springtime so all flowers will be in bloom, and for the opening shot the use of butterflies is essential. As Grandma serenely cultivates her plants, her delightful descendants approach her quietly, and articulately ask her...

Boy [blond and about nine years old]: What are you doing, Grandma?
Grandma: I'm feeding my garden.
Girl [also blonde and about seven years old]: I didn't know that gardens needed food, Grandma.
Grandma: Of course they do. Just like I fed your Mummy and your Mummy feeds you, my beautiful flowers need nourishment too.
Boy and Girl [together]: Ohhh. We love you, Grandma.

Grandma: And I love you too.
[Music swells as loving looks are exchanged and Grandma hugs the children and the children hug Grandma. Cocker spaniel enters the frame, leaping joyfully and making everybody laugh.]
Grandma: You must all be hungry.
Boy and Girl [together]: Oh yes, Grandma.
Grandma: Come inside, I've made hot chocolate and gingerbread men for you. *[Turns to spaniel]* And there's a big, juicy bone for you.

As they all make their way towards Grandma's charming, sandstone home, the camera tilts down to reveal her meticulously maintained gardening tools, her basket for collecting flowers, her well-worn, oiled leather gardening gloves and a bag of the product. The music ends here. The logo now appears on the screen in silence: Australian Chicken Manure—for all that's pure in your garden!

You, you make me feel brand-new...

Australian Chicken Manure—Proposal No. 3

(ANTI-ADS NEVER HAVE TITLES)

We anticipate that this proposal could well be the most expensive one but, as you will see, the travel involved for all of us, with our assistants, will be arduous but all-important to the concept we've devised.

The theme of this campaign is musical and visual, with very little dialogue—but incredibly relevant. With a music bed of Johannes Brahms's Alto Rhapsody Opus 53, we will present a plethora of images appropriate to, but not in such an overbearing way as to be detrimental to the product.

The opening picture will be of a big red kangaroo bounding across the Simpson Desert with Ayers Rock standing majestically in the background. Next we'll see a helicopter shot tracing the coastline from Perth to Broome. From here, we'll drop in on a corroborree in Arnhem Land and then a quick dash across Queensland for a three-second underwater exploration of the Great Barrier Reef.

Interspersed with these images of Australia will be visuals, hereinafter known as 'the chicken content'. This part of the concept is targeted at the family situation. Suggested ideas are: two or three fluffy, little, yellow chicks nuzzling into the necks of a couple of adorable toddlers; a good-looking young mum serving a succulent, home-cooked roast chicken dinner to her equally good-looking husband and children; a nineteenth-century homestead, painted white, with a good-looking, country wife standing on the veranda, throwing feed to a group of clean, healthy, good-looking and beautifully groomed, free-range chickens.

Finally, scattered throughout the Australian images and 'chicken content' will be subtle references to manure. These must be handled with extreme delicacy. Some recommendations for dealing with this somewhat sensitive part of the production are: a wide shot of potato farmers in Tasmania (not Cliff Young in Victoria) raking the soil; a very wide shot of vineyard workers in the Barossa Valley digging around the vines; a very, very wide shot of horticulturalists in Melbourne's Fitzroy Gardens hoeing and spreading. It is important that we are never truly aware of what is being raked, dug, hoed or spread into the soil!

For the closing sequence, we go to the forecourt of the Sydney Opera House with the Harbour Bridge, ferries, hydrofoils *et al*, in the background. Here we find Elle MacPherson sitting alone at a table, sipping iced water. A dinky-di Australian farmer (dressed in appropriate attire of moleskins, Akubra hat, R. M. Williams' boots) strolls past Elle with a bag of the product over his broad shoulder (careful not to display product name

87

too prominently). She turns to camera and says, 'I had a chicken once'.

So whether it's Finger Lickin' Good, or A Natural Part of Life, you can't Leave Home Without It. Advertising— Ask for it by name!

19

Recycling our lives

'Who's looking after Planet Earth?'—
An alien's report

As we freefall towards the end of the twentieth century, it is becoming clear to us that perhaps our daring jump into the abyss of technology for reasons of economic and sustainable growth, or a sometimes misguided evaluation of our world's needs, was an unfortunate error of judgment.

In our efforts to become richer and lead more comfortable lives, we have managed, firstly, to rip a hole in the ozone layer which should slowly bring us all to boiling point—and, if we are lucky enough not to all drop dead of heat exhaustion or skin cancer, the air pollution will most likely finish us off. Now, before you go rushing out to a gas mask sale, make sure you can colour-coordinate it with the life-jacket you'll need for surviving in the sea of toxic waste!

We have become 'green' obsessed. Suddenly, we are working ourselves into a biodegradable lather of recycling, replanting and re-just about everything else. Now, just suppose, we Friends of the Earth were being observed by some non-earthly beings of advanced intelligence...

THE PLACE:	The Planet of Vegetation, in the Green Galaxy
THE TIME:	Now
THE ALIENS:	The Vegheads, a race of highly intelligent investigative reporters
THE REPORT	An in-depth survey of the Earth's environment. What in the world have they been doing?!

Valda Veghead, Chairveg of the Verdant Advisory Group: Order, order, the centennial meeting of VAG is now in session. On the agenda for today are three reports which have been compiled over the last few Earth years. The findings on the domestic sector will be presented by Verity Vendt, who has risked life and limb to bring the truth of the situation home to us. The controversial summary on the industrial sector will be in the capable hands of Violet Vinch, and I promise you she didn't shy away from this one. And, finally, the all-important conclusions on the government sector will be explained to us by Vonnie Villesee, and, let me tell you, this needs some explaining.
Vegheads: [Murmuring excitedly] Voom, voom, voom, voom...
Valda: Yes, yes, should be quite a day. But just before I call upon our first speaker, I would like to thank my lovely husband, Victor, and all the gentlevegs in the Auxiliary, for providing us with the beautiful platters of vegetable scones for refreshments later.
Vegheads: Voom, voom, voom, voom, voom...
Valda: Okay, okay, settle down. Now, please give a big VAG welcome to Vs Verity Vendt.
Verity Vendt: As you know, I was assigned to Planet Earth for some years to investigate their care of the environment, domestically speaking. I'd have to say I found it very interesting. They are very proud of an invention called 'plastic' and they use it for everything. It's used

to package food, to store something they call 'garbage', and I even saw a baby earthling wearing pants made from it.

Vegheads: Voom, voom, voom, voom, voom...

Verity: I know, I know. But, believe me, I'm telling you the truth! Next, they drink from cups formed from polystyrene. Remember that stuff? It was outlawed here nearly five million years ago. And, that's not the end of it. They use it for packaging everything from washing machines to snow peas, and I even witnessed an earthling buying a plastic bag full of polystyrene balls. Upon inquiring, I learned that these balls are used as stuffing for a strange sitting device they call a 'beanbag'. Oddly enough, they like to leave a small opening in a seam to allow these balls to escape throughout their homes.

A Veghead: Vs Verity, what is 'garbage'?

Verity: Good question! We have never known of this on the Planet of Vegetation, but the earthlings are full of it. They've lived with it since their time began, but apparently the problem has reached its peak this Earth century. They have always been a throwaway society. Only now are they learning what we have known for twenty billion years—reduce, reuse, recycle. Until recently, they were burying glass, paper and cardboard, ferrous and non-ferrous metals, and piles of their beloved invention, plastic.

A Veghead: Burying! But, how can anything green grow on top of all that junk?

Verity: Absolutely! As I was saying, they are only now just learning to reduce their plastics, reuse their metals and glass, and recycle their paper products.

Vegheads: [Thrilled murmuring] Va, va, va, va, va, va, va, va, va...

Verity: As on many planets, it's the women who are leading the way in caring for the environment. The female Earthlings have taken to recycling with a vengeance. Their cooking places are lined with receptacles

labelled 'tins', 'glass', 'plastic', and 'paper'. But the most exciting development is that they have learned to use the compost heap—not just for garden rubbish but for kitchen waste as well.
Vegheads: Va, va, va, va, va, va ...
Verity: In closing, I would just like to let you know also that besides this I investigated the domestic activity at a number of supermarkets. The Earthling women have taken up the cause of conservation there too. They are now taking great care in selecting cleaning agents which are friendly to nature. Unfortunately, most of these products are still in plastic bottles but the girls are at least more aware and making an effort. Now, if they could only get the shopping home without their most dreadful invention, the plastic carry bag!
A Veghead: Question, Vs Verity. What is a 'supermarket'?
Verity: Sorry, out of time ... but you could see me later!
Valda: Thank you, Verity. Another great Earthling insight. Now, just before I introduce our next speaker, I'm pleased to tell you, the long-awaited Vegball rematch between the Veghead Beans and the Veghead Sprouts has been scheduled for next weekend. Hope to see you all there.
Vegheads: Vim, vim, vim, vim, vim, vim ...
Valda: Continuing our comprehensive examination of Planet Earth, the next spokesveg, Violet Vinch, will report on the industrial sector. Vi ...
Violet Vinch: Shame, Earth, shame! Who's looking after the environment? I'll say it here, I'll say it now, and in case you don't believe me, I'll say it again. The barrage of industrial waste that continues to be dumped on this fragile, once-green globe is of such disastrous proportions that I pray it will never be witnessed on our Planet of Vegetation. I have never seen destruc ...
Vegheads: Voom, voom, voom.
Valda: Would you like to take a break, Violet?
Violet: No, no, I must go on. I have never seen destruction

like it. Admittedly, my first Earth stop was in an area they call Alaska, where they were trying to recover their world's largest oil spill from a big, ugly, sea-going vessel. It was horrible and the authorities I interviewed told me the damage to the environment would not be repaired in their lifetime.
Vegheads: Voom, voom.
Violet: I then took an overall look at their attitude towards their native vegetation. There is evidence that there was once an abundance of greenery but they seem to have adopted a mentality of 'chop it down and chip it'. The destruction and waste of trees everywhere would appal you!
A Veghead: But how do they expect to survive?
Violet: Well asked! We Vegheads learned millennia ago that we need trees to live because they clean the air we breathe. But the Earthlings are only beginning to understand this concept.
A Veghead: That's okay in principle, but what are they doing about it?
Violet: In one region, known as Australia, a little man with a round head covered in silver waves, proudly announced the planting of a billion trees before the end of their century.
The Vegheads: Whaaaatt, only a billion? Voom, voom.
Violet: But they still haven't successfully addressed their problem of toxic wastes. However, to explain to you the intricacies and difficulties behind this dilemma, I will hand you over to my colleague, Vonnie Villesee, who will attempt to describe 'government'.
Vonnie Villesee: Thank you, Violet. Congratulations on your report. We all know how involved you became and how difficult it was for you. But now to my findings. As stated before, my brief was to examine the government sector, and, oh dear, what an absorbing and mystifying area this has shown itself to be. Although the care of the environment is a universal concern, I

decided to focus my study on the island continent of Australia. The inhabitants of this land are particularly prone to 'garbage'.
The Vegheads: Voom, voom, voom, voom, voom.
Vonnie: Government controls on the disposal of industrial wastes appear to be a little lacking. Time and time again, I saw polluted waterways, man-made barren areas known as 'toxic dumps', and hazardous chemicals stored in a dangerously cavalier manner. Upon interviewing a number of Earthlings, I discovered that the general population is actually quite concerned about the situation and are urging for something to be done. Their catchcry was 'Go ask them blokes in Canberra', so I did.
A Veghead: Question, Vs Vonnie, what is a 'Canberra'?
Vonnie: [Laughing] Va, va, va, va. It is a 'meeting place', and another meaning for it is 'women's breasts' which often causes some confusion for the powers that live there. As a city, it's like nothing we've ever seen before. Its basic layout resembles a learn-to-drive school or a mini golf course. On a small rise in this flat metropolis there stands a monument to the Earthling authorities called Parliament House. This is where 'the blokes' are housed. They were 'sitting' when I arrived but sometime later they stood up and I was ushered in to see the little man with a round head covered in silver waves. He greeted me warmly, listened intently to my claims, stated his deep concern, and pledged his support. Three minutes later, standing outside his door, I bumped into an unusual-looking Earthling, devoid of silver or any other kind of waves, gyrating down the hall and singing, 'How Can We Sleep When Our Beds Are Burning?'.
Vegheads: Voom, voom, va, va, va, vim.
Vonnie: Yes, it is a catchy tune, isn't it. For quite some time, I chatted to this intelligent Earthling, who explained to me the peculiar Australian syndrome of 'Too Much Red Tape and Not Enough Action'. It appears

that there are so many levels of government with a finger in the environmental pie that it's very hard for practical results to be achieved. The great gyrating one then invited me to a 'gig' and disappeared.

Vegheads: Vim, vim, vim, vim, vim, vim.

Vonnie: In summary, the care of the Earth's environment is obviously very complex but manageable if tackled diligently and now. They have no time to waste and they are starting to realise, 'It's Not Easy Being Green'.

Vegheads: Va, va, va, va, va, va, va.

Valda: Thank you, speakers. Now, hasn't that given us all a lot to think about? I know you must all be feeling ready for some refreshment. The vegetable scones will be served in the Green Room in five minutes. I hope you enjoy the musical accompaniment provided by the Reduce, Reuse, Recycle Chamber Orchestra. Remember, the food must be consumed quickly or it disintegrates and recycles itself!

20

Give way to the right—
It may be your mother
Driving: a woman's view

'I bought my wife a new car. She called me and said there was water in the carburettor. I said "Where's the car?" She said, "In the lake".' HENNY YOUNGMAN

'**B**loody women drivers!' 'Where'd you get your licence, lady? In a raffle?!' And on and on they go. Second only to mothers-in-law, women drivers cop the greatest number of disparaging comments, jokes and insults. But what about having a look at it from the female point of view?

When you become the proud holder of a driver's licence, you discover that the rules of the road bear absolutely no resemblance to anything that you may have been previously taught about social values and behaviour. Common courtesy, respect for your elders, thoughtfulness toward others, and 'Don't use bad language' are all principles instilled in us from a very early age.

So, why is it that the minute most men sit behind the wheel of a car, the gentlemanly standards learned at their mother's knee fly out the window faster than thay can hurl abuse out of it?

For instance, when little boys are growing up they are taught how important it is to let someone know where they are going. So why can't they remember this now and use their indicator to let us, in the traffic, know where they are going?

Another annoying attitude to drivers of the female persuasion is that, regardless of our age or driving skills, we are all lumped into the category of being geriatrics. Most of us have been 'You silly old bag' since the age of eighteen!

Somewhere in the cycle of motorised evolution, men have lost the ability to 'give way' in a line of traffic. Perhaps this relates back to some primal need to be the leader of the pack. How often have you attempted to legally change lanes only to be blocked by an unyielding vehicle being driven by a rogue male steadfastly refusing even to acknowledge your presence, let alone let you in? For pity's sake, all we're talking here is one car length? Real smart, macho man!

Forget about waving your arms, getting hot under the collar and performing Marcel Marceau mime—it gets you nowhere in this situation. We, however, have found one foolproof method of breaking into the line of traffic. Wind your window down and call out in your best Maggie Thatcher voice, 'Excuse me, may I get in front of you? Thank you!' They seem to find this personal contact so threatening that it stuns them into silent submission. Go on, give it a try!

Bad language emanating from the interior of many cars is another subject that warrants some scrutiny here. Even the most timid among us, who under normal circumstances have never been known to raise our voices in anger, have found ourselves with our heads spinning and spewing invective more suited to Linda Blair in *The Exorcist*. We obviously feel protected by the confines of the car because this behaviour anywhere else would get us prosecuted. Can you imagine the reaction to 'F .. off, you silly old bugger' on a crowded escalator in Myer?

Another angle to our 'confines of the car' theory is that many—okay, we feel forced to say it here—*men*, feel that being alone in their vehicle renders them wholly invisible. Believing they can't be seen, they then proceed to exhibit the most extraordinary forms of behaviour. These antics can range from a sedate drum-roll on the steering wheel to an all-out impersonation, on the dashboard, of Bruce Springsteen and his entire E Street Band; from a quiet chat with themselves to a full-on rehearsal of the shouting match they are about to have with the wife when they get home; and, the most disconcerting of all, anything from an absent-minded dab at the corner of their eye to the astonishing trick of completely losing their index finger up their nose!

Speaking of noses, something that really gets up ours is the recent popular use of signs, bumper stickers and assorted 'decorative' paraphernalia. As it is, our car windows are forever advertising where we bought it, where and when it was serviced, and what month it was registered. Why some people feel it necessary to add to this clobber is beyond us. Who cares if you'd 'Rather Be Snorkelling'? Who wants to know that 'Old Plumbers Don't Die, They Just Go Down the Drain'? And, who really knows for sure if 'Jesus Cares'? We feel certain that Edsel Ford never meant his bumper to be used like this!

Our award for the Most Aggravating Automotive Accessory, however, goes to those ridiculous 'Baby On Board' signs. What's the point? Is it presumed that we intentionally drive into the back of cars but, on seeing this 'B.O.B.' warning, we will swerve around this vehicle and head for one without that protection?

On a final note, a word to the road traffic authorities. It's about these new driver's licences with photographs. Come on, guys, let's talk seriously here. If we are to be stuck with these photos for years at a time, then you're going to have to provide us with better facilities. We don't mind having to bring along our own costumes, but you've got to come to the party too. We suggest, at the very least, a make-up and hair stylist, but if that's a budgetary problem for your department, perhaps you could see your way clear to hanging up a mirror in each branch office!

We're not pretending to be experts in motoring or that all women are perfect drivers, but we feel it's our right to defend ourselves against the criticism that has been regularly doled out to us.

It hasn't always been easy. Some of us have had to battle gigantic genetic flaws when it came to learning to drive. My mother, Mona Mann, taught me. And this was a woman who had devised a way of getting around Melbourne by only turning left because, as she used to say, 'Most accidents happen when people are turning right!'

21

The ever-changing face of functions

A partygiver's guide to gracious gaiety

Having dealt with the complexities of obligatory family functions in Chapter 5, we think it's time to get back to our own lives and start some serious partygiving. Gather up your best buddies and boogie!

This kind of bash does not need a reason for being, but it is important to note a few basic guidelines to ensure your bop is not a flop.

What type of party do you want? Is it going to be a cocktail party? ('Nothing fancy, dahling, just a few nibbles and some drinkie-poohs.') Is it going to be a sit-down formal dinner? ('Yes, dahling, five courses, heaps of cutlery, the whole she-bang.') Is it going to be a buffet? ('Now come on, dahlings, stand back, there's plenty for everyone.') Is it going to be a barbecue? ('You know, dahling, steaks, snags and shish kebabs.') Is it going to be an intimate supper for two? ('Just picture it, dahling, candlelight, wine and moi.') Or is it an all-out, full-on, bop-till-you-drop party (BYO everything)?

Once you have determined the type of party you want to give, the other social components fall into place.

Questions like what type of guest, how to dress, what food to serve, what games to play and how to behave are easily sorted out from here on in.

When compiling their guest lists, prize-winning party givers understand the words 'the right mix'. Many a best friend has had to be sacrificed on the dinner party altar for the sake of a successful blend of table talk. Your worst nightmares will almost certainly come true if you dare to seat your boss's new wife, who has recently returned from her annual pilgrimage to the Dalai Lama, next to your girlfriend's dickhead husband. (Imagine the look on the poor woman's face as he regales her with stories of his latest weekend obsession of acting out war games in the bush.)

The next question is, what look are you going for fashionwise? Again, depending on the type of party and the type of guest, this is a variable. However, you can't go wrong with dressing 'middle of the road'. We're not talking mediocre or drab here—we advocate a sense of style at all times. For instance, a summer barbecue, out the back and poolside, should see you in a smart swimsuit (not necessarily a one-piece if you think you can get away with something less!) and a colourful sarong of tropical design.

And, if He's still sporting a Safari suit and long socks—dump him!

Cocktail parties no longer require the wearing of those funny little veiled hats called 'fascinators'—that is, unless you want to strain your daiquiri while you are drinking it! The appropriate attire for a formal sit-down dinner party is very much up to your own discretion. A full-length, silk shantung Fairy Princess dress, with pearl-beaded bodice and crystal-detailed sleeves is a little over the top these days—unless you're living in a soap opera, in which case you'd be underdressed!

For an intimate candlelit supper for two, your choice of garb is only as limited as your imagination. However, the flicker of candlelight on a nude form has been known to work a treat!

How to conduct yourself on all occasions must always be considered carefully. Remember, as hostess you set the example to the rest. Here are just a few pointers to help you along the way. To begin with, don't get too drunk too early—it's important that you serve the main course before midnight and are still able to recognise any latecomers! When allocating places at table, put divorced couples at opposite ends to keep china breakage to a minimum. At large functions, don't be caught out talking to your spouse for too long— it's social suicide! And, if during some celebration, you find yourself sitting beside the Pope, don't call him Jack or even Pope John Paul. His correct callsign is His Holiness. (Never know when you might need this one!)

If you are a single hostess, it's not necessary today to invite a date for yourself, although it does help to have someone there to assist you with attending to the guests. If, on the other hand, you are a hostess with a partner, it is advisable to issue him with a job description before the invited freeloaders arrive. There is nothing more annoying than watching your partner be the best guest at his own party!

Party games can be of some use as a welcome diversion if the pace of the evening becomes sluggish and, dare we say it, boring. In days gone by, there were charades and Spin the Bottle and, more recently, Trivial Pursuit and Pictionary have invaded the party scene, but because of the emotions these games can arouse, a hostess must keep all activities under strict control. A favourite of ours is a little game called 'Get Knotted'. On 'Go', everyone closes their eyes, runs into the centre of the room and grabs the first two hands they come across. Next, they open their eyes and try to untangle themselves without letting go of the hands they are holding. Players get into all sorts of difficulties as they climb over and under bodies, between legs, around shoulders—all over each other. It really livens things up!

All good things must come to an end, but why is it that some guests have trouble seeing it that way? Invariably, the lingerers turn out to be the 'and Friend' who are now so drunk they've forgotten who they came with, and their partner has departed in disgust much earlier, anyway. One of the often suggested ways of dealing with this problem is to turn off the drinks. However, our experience of this is that these hangers-on are extremely ingenious when it comes to artificial stimuli. At one function we organised recently a small group of survivors, led by our very own partners, had resorted to sucking the helium out of the balloons used for decoration and talking in Donald Duck voices in a pathetic attempt to prolong the evening's festivities. It didn't work. The ringleaders were sent to bed and the others were shown the door!

If you follow even some of these guidelines, the glittering prize of the perfect party will be within your grasp. But never despair; even we self-appointed gurus of gracious gaiety have our moments of anguish. The idea of the party excites us. We carefully invite the guests. We plan the menu perfectly. We organise the games down to the minutest detail. The vases are bursting with fresh flowers. The cuisine is simmering to a nouvelle in the kitchen. It's usually around 4 p.m. when it suddenly hits you. 'What the bloody hell am I doing this for?' Don't panic. It happens to all of us. If you can ride out this moment of angst, things can only get better.

Relax. Be gracious. Be gay. It's your party—and you won't cry 'cause you don't want to!

22

*O*ut to shop!

Everything you ever wanted to know about shopping but were afraid to ask

Since Adam first gave Eve the original gift voucher from the Garden of Eden Emporium, the science of good shopping has been researched, discussed, lectured about, and examined right down to the last minute detail. With all this analysis, we have yet to see an adequate interpretation of shopping psychology.

So, after much active research on our part, we now feel equipped to bring to you our definitive index on this subject of vital importance. When on your next spree, you may find our catalogue of some use.

*O*ur Guide to Shoppers

1   The Born to Shop Shopper. This species we can relate to extremely well. Their common characteristics are an enthusiasm for buying anything, depression when arms are empty and wallet is full, and psychic foresight of new shopping complexes before the foundations are even laid. Top marks to this class.

They're a credit to the breed. If you are lucky enough to be shopping in the presence of one of these masters, don't waste this opportunity of a lifetime!

2 The Get In, Grab It, and Get Out Shopper. Sometimes known as the I Hate to Shop Shopper. This breed we find a little strange but, sadly, it is quite common. These poor, unfortunate creatures loathe and despise every detail of the shopping experience. They will enter shops only after intense coercion. Realising they have no choice, they adopt the commando raid approach: race in, rifle through, remunerate and retreat!

3 The Analytical Shopper. This animal can be a right, royal pain in the arse. Their plaintive squawk, 'Yes, but what is it made of . . . ? can be heard from the recesses of changing rooms around Australia. Particularly extreme cases have been known to ask for a CSIRO analysis. Recommended treatment for this acute condition is a short, sharp smack in the face!

4 The Impulse Shopper. Closely resembling, but not to be confused with, The Bargain Shopper. These two related species often feed off one another, which can cause enormous problems. On the one hand, The Impulse Shopper can have the ability to execute a purchase with style and flair, for example buying a Dutch-pink Mercedes 300SE when their driver's licence has been suspended. In contrast, The Bargain Shopper is sometimes known to be a touch pedestrian in their choice of product, for instance buying twenty-four pairs of size 12 plastic sandals in July 'because they were so cheap!'

5 The Specific Object Shopper. Sadly, most of us have been guilty of behaviour displayed by this category at one point or another. How many times have you headed off merrily into the shopping precinct saying, 'I'll know it when I see it!' Be honest. How often have you seen it? Never! What a ridiculous idea.

You were beaten before you began. All you wanted was a simple, white skirt and you've come home with three pairs of brown shoes. We of Category One learned this lesson years ago!

6   The Window Shopper. Otherwise known as The Browser. This is one of the more despicable examples of the genus. Let loose, these can be a menace to the entire consuming community. They only look; they never buy. They are annoying enough in the everyday shopping experience but to encounter one of them in an after-Christmas sale can be downright hazardous. The number of injuries sustained by bona fide buyers while rushing to the cash counter, clutching their bargains, when they crash into these itinerant browsers who have *stopped to look* is a disgrace. There should be a law against them!

7   The Lazy Shopper. This group is quite ingenious in its approach to the act of shopping, but we appreciate that it might not be for everybody. It involves a best friend with a driver's licence. The

theory is that the best friend drives slowly along the street while you (the lazy one) view the merchandise on display through a pair of binoculars. If you spot a little something you simply must have, the best friend then idles kerbside while you sprint in to acquire it. This method of amassing goods does have some drawbacks—petrol fumes have been outlawed inside David Jones!

To aid your understanding of this amazing breed of Shoppers, it is worthwhile taking a look at some of their habitats.

1   Boutique. Usually a small shop, run by small women and stocking extremely small sizes.
2   Supermarket. Large shop, usually providing a full range of food products which can only be gathered in a conveyance with a wonky wheel.
3   Hypermarket. An even larger shop, providing a full range of everything from quail's eggs to men's underwear, from a wafflemaker to a three-edged shovel. Plenty of parking!
4   Emporium. Another large shop usually selling a great variety of articles—and we do mean great! Paradise for buyers, not browsers.
5   Shopping plaza. Usually a combination of all the above and commonly worshipped as a sacred shrine.

For those interested in becoming part of this elite group, it would be remiss of us not to point out its natural enemy—The Shop Assistant!

There are exceptions—very few—but generally we have found these adversaries to be formidable. Their extraordinary behaviour is far too complex to detail fully at this time, but some of their more idiosyncratic traits include:

1   Their refusal to serve you, and their ability to ignore

you completely before, during and after your transaction.
2. Their irritating habit of abandoning you, usually stripped naked, in a cubicle surrounded by clothing in every size but the one you want.
3. Their insistence that you struggle into a size 6, strapless gown which can be fastened only by breaking two of your ribs and cutting off your circulation. This is always capped off by the antagonist bleating, 'Gee, that looks nice on you!'

In spite of attempts to cull this opposing group, they remain a part of shopping life. But don't be put off—the joy of buying makes it all worthwhile.

One ray of light at the end of the shopping tunnel is the opportunity to do it all from the comfort of your own home by mail order. Executed according to its design specifications, for some, this consumer experience can be the ultimate one. You drool over the catalogue, you dial and demand your choice, you dally by the garden gate and await your delivery. It's all so ducky!

But for us there is nothing quite like the real thing. The roar of the cash register, the smell of the shop—you can't beat it.

Shopping can be great therapy. Many a thorny problem can be resolved while picking your way through the hair accessories bar at Myer. A good buy is a tremendous healer. It's good for your psyche, it's good for your soul, and it's fabulous for your wardrobe!

Not so much bankrupt as a little financially embarrassed

Women—The real financiers of the nineties

'Come on, John, why is it always my job to speak to the bank manager?'

It may never rate a mention in the *Australian Financial Review*, but, without women playing the role of Fiscal Brokers in Charge of Home Affairs, the economy of the country would be further down the plughole than it is already.

The days of the 'little woman' being allowed to budget only with the housekeeping money are fading fast. Today's 'housekeeper' has to be an expert in negotiation of bank loans, credit card management, the discharging of debtors, the juggling of creditors, chartered accounting, the laws of taxation, supermarket investment, and organising the staff picnic!

And that's all before she does the dishes and makes the beds!

A Day in the Life of a Fiscal Broker in Charge of Home Affairs

7.30 a.m. She awakes and immediately checks her diary. A busy day ahead of her, but she's known it to be worse.

7.35 a.m. Beds made.

7.36 a.m. Prepares breakfast, referees hostilities at table.

8.00 a.m. Farewells the troops, plants the obligatory peck on His cheek, does the dishes, vacs the family room, and puts a load on.

9.00 a.m. The Bank Liaison and Liquidity Officer's hat is pulled snugly on for the first meeting of the day.

9.30 a.m. She's on time for the appointment and is ushered into one of those dreadful little glass offices where everyone can read her lips and then blab her business to all and sundry. Next she faces the humiliation of the Loans Officer being young enough to offer her a seat on a bus. (She seems to recall his face in her son's football team photo.) She signs on the dotted line. She leaves the bank, safe in the knowledge that she has borrowed enough to repay the bank the money that she already owes them.

10.00 a.m. She joins the queue waiting for teller service. (She is now a past master at ignoring the lip-reader's stares.) She hopes to cash a cheque. She digs in for a long wait. She has learned from her years in the home banking business that if she waits long enough, a computer will 'go down' and a balance of her account will be rendered impossible.

11.45 a.m. She leaves bank with cash in hand.

11.47 a.m. Arrival at the supermarket. She pulls on her Investment Co-Ordinator for Home Economics cap.

12.33 p.m. Arrival at the checkout queue.

1.33 p.m. Arrival at the cash register. The race begins between her mental arithmetic and the flying fingers of the checkout chick. Will she be forced to jettison anything? What doesn't the family 'need' this week? She holds her breath. The total appears. It's down to the wire but she'll make it this time.

2.06 p.m. She changes her chapeau to that of Plastic Credit Consultant. Her mission is to collect for Him five litres of paint, one plank and two ladders. The trick here is to buy these with a credit card. Another meaning for 'plastic' is 'manageable' so this should be easy. She watches the salesman anxiously as he checks her line of credit by phone. Will she pass the test? Or will he return wielding a giant pair of scissors and demanding the instant destruction of her card? Slightly panicked, she prepares a game plan. She'll only buy one ladder! He returns. He smiles. She's in the clear!

2.42 p.m. After unloading the car, she dons her steel-reinforced Accounts Payable and Receivable helmet. The asset shuffle begins. 'Now, let's see...' If so-and-so paid up, she could pay a bit more off the Bankcard. Or, if such-and-such came through with some money, she could get Telecom off her back. And, if that other cheque really is in the mail, she could pay off the washing machine. Round and round it goes.

3.15 p.m. She's still on the phone. It's the Accountant. Will she balance the books in time for him to do the tax? (No worries. She's got nothing else to do!)

3.28 p.m. The phone rings again. He was just wondering if she had had time yet to pick up his dry-cleaning.

3.30 p.m. Picks up kids from school. Drives one to swimming, one to music, one to football. She stops for petrol, making sure she doesn't exceed the $4.83 she has left in her purse.

4.20 p.m. She's home again, this time with the dry-cleaning. Shells peas while continuing to asset-shuffle on phone.

4.35 p.m. She's back in the car. Collects kids. Then home.

6.15 p.m. Dinner is served. Referees hostilities at table.

7.00 p.m. Organises dishes, bath and bed.
7.30 p.m. Settles down for a relaxing night of balancing the books.
8.47 p.m. Asks Him to turn down the volume on the television. Goes back to the search for the missing $7.23.
11.30 p.m. Locks up. Turns out the lights. Crawls into bed. As she drifts into sleep, she promises to buy herself a cheap pocket-sized calculator to relieve some of the supermarket checkout stress!
11.35 p.m. She dreams she is a mouse on a treadmill.

24

If you're going to stick it out, girls, then firm it up!

The corporate handshake—An introduction to a new career

Since the dawn of time, the corporate jungle has reverberated with the sound of the executive Tarzans of this world. Their bellowing has deafened big business for centuries. But with the onset of the nineties, the Janes are crooning their way into new careers.

In the past, if you found yourself at a loose end at the age of twenty, with—heaven help us!—no prospect of marriage on the horizon, you had to 'get a job'.

Thoughts of financial independence, a sense of freedom and questions like, 'How much you got in your Christmas Club?' flooded into your mind. Your own place, your own set of wheels, your own telephone—all there for the taking!

So, what were the options? Let's see. Secretary, teacher, nurse or nun? 'But I want to be Investment Manager in Charge of Foreign Currency for the Reserve Bank. Where do I apply?'

The fact of the matter was, you didn't! But you could apply to be a bank teller—well, until you got married, anyway.

Thankfully, things are now changing and career choices for women are opening up enormously. You can now be advised financially, legally and gynaecologically without ever setting eyes on a man, if you so choose. Consequently, in the corporate jungle of today, Jane is no longer sitting in the grass hut waiting for Tarzan to swing in with a bunch of bananas. She is out there with him, side by side, fighting the person-eating crocodiles!

Now that the Sisters are out there doing it for themselves, they must keep a good supply of chalk so their grip doesn't slip as they climb up the corporate ladder. The incidentals of tertiary qualifications, impeccable training, and hands-on experience are only a drop in the big business bucket. For the gals to flourish in the rarefied atmosphere of the executive toilet, they need to remember a couple of things.

There has been some importance placed on power dressing, by some powerful women in some powerful positions. We're not sure how it works exactly, but one thing we do know is that shoulder-pads are best used to broaden the line of your shoulders and not to improve the size of your bust or to give you very fat elbows! Velcro is definitely the way to go!

One last word on shoulder-pads—be cautious of the size you choose and, above all, do not go over the top, otherwise you will find yourself having to walk sideways into the boardroom! This doesn't do much for your credibility!

First impressions pack a powerful punch. So if you're aiming for the Business Woman of the Nineties Award, and choose to adopt the now in-vogue handshake for greeting all and sundry, there are a few basic rules.

As the phenomenon of female handshaking is relatively recent, we are sorry to observe that some recipients are intimidated by its very presence.

Don't you be intimidated—don't dangle it, hold it

steady and keep it there! Otherwise, the greeting could be reduced to something akin to really bad street theatre.

Hand presentation is important. The angle of extension determines how it is received. There is nothing worse than a hand coming towards you, turned in such a way that you're not sure whether to shake it, dodge it or lean over and kiss it!

Finally, firmness of grip. The grasp of the limp mullet, otherwise known as the 'wet fish' handshake, is not a pleasant experience for anyone. However, the other extreme, which we call the Arnie Schwarzenegger Clutch, is not a good idea either. It's important to leave them with enough fingers intact to sign the deal!

We realise these manual manoeuvres may require some practice. To our knowledge, there are no courses available for this at the present time. But the corporate handshake can be practised and achieved quite successfully in the privacy of your own home. The family pet can be useful (preferably a dog or cat as you don't want to be caught shaking the canary's claw). Failing this, a rolled-up tea-towel will do the trick. But the best idea of all is to experiment on your poor unsuspecting relatives at the Sunday roast!

25

When your software becomes floppy and your mouse has lost its byte

Surviving the technological age

Life has become just one big 'plug-in'! Even the simplest of tasks these days cannot be attempted without the turning on of at least a couple of modern-day machines. We write letters on computers; we send instant messages around the world by fax machine; we chat on the telephone in the kitchen, in the office, in our car, or by the pool; we can conduct business for days without actually speaking to anyone in the flesh, via telephone answering machines; and we can be posted for a year to Mawson Base, Antarctica, and still be able to catch up with all of our favourite soaps through the convenience of a VCR.

We have become a press-button society. Gone are the days of the knob!

For example, let's take the humble television. It's no longer a case of just turn it on or off. We now have an assortment of buttons to press on a gismo that is not even attached to the set. And, as if that's not enough to contend with, VCRs (now as common in every Australian household as the wooden spoon) can also be operated with a handheld contraption. Sometimes one can find oneself with a box full of extra remote-control units, particularly if one's television/VCR has been stolen a couple of times. For some inexplicable reason, the burglars always take the television and the tape machine and leave the gadgets behind!

Banking is another button-operated area that is leaving us, the electronically dyslexic dills, behind. How pleasant it used to be when everything was on a personal level. The trip to the bank was a real outing. You'd stand in the queue, usually for hours, but that was okay because it gave you time to chat to Ruby from next door or Mr Hardwicke from Hardwicke's Haberdashery. Then it would be your turn at the window. Cheryl or Narelle would greet you warmly, discuss the weather and complete your transactions competently.

With the advent of the confounded automatic teller machines, the soul has gone from banking. It's ripped the heart right out of it. You now stand in a queue with people you don't know, in all kinds of weather, desperately trying to remember your PIN number, and hunching over the machine to protect your hard-earned cash from the lurking, marauding hordes around you.

What we wouldn't give now to see the return of the smiling teller's face, the sensible bank uniform and that nice pair of cork wedgies!

This brings us to numbers, for the technological age is also a digital age. Apart from learning the telephone numbers for our home, car and beeper, we also have to know numbers for our fax machine, our driver's licence, our car registration, our Medicare, our automatic bank accounts, the stations on our car radio, and—the most irritating of all—our video club number.

The entertaining art of music has even been taken over by electronic engineering. Why waste money on violin lessons when you can achieve the same effect by plugging in your Lowery organ with built-in string section and drum machine?

Obviously, this electronic style of music has become very popular in business. The recent telephone practice of using muzak to entertain the long-suffering customer while on 'hold' is a particularly aggravating one. How many times can one be assailed by Barry Manilow's melodic tones crooning that he 'Can't Smile Without You'?

Listening to music has also become computerised. The clunk of a big hunk of vinyl onto the turntable, the comfort of the 'sshh sshh sshh' as you waited for the first track to start, and the thrill of getting a good ball of fluff off the needle are but glorious memories. So, now when you want to be swept away by your favourite ABBA album, you reach for the record only to discover it has shrunk to a CD (literally a compact disc). You slide in the CD, you switch on the amplifier, and you turn up the speakers, being careful to balance the bass with the treble and the woofers with the tweeters. Now try singing along to 'Mama Mia'!

Today, the big guns in the technological takeover are home computers and fax machines. The day is fast approaching where sufferers of agoraphobia will no longer be phobic: there will be nowhere to fear because there will be nowhere to go. Banking, shopping, reading newspapers, medical information, and legal advice will soon all be available by courtesy of the home computer. Unfortunately, this will be of no use to us scientific ninnies. Still, we can always employ our eight-year-olds as computer operators (sure beats a paper round for pocket money!).

Home fax machines (we love 'em!) are fast becoming the postmen of the future. No fear of your dog chomping into them! However, as with all new-fangled contraptions, many people do experience massive operational problems. The first rule of thumb is to trust your fax. Some users are so worried and downright afraid of the cavernous unknown that they refuse to release their vice-like grip on their documents and end up in a vicious tug-of-war with the great sucking machine. These doubting dummies, who have caused a malfunction, then blame the machine and declare it 'user unfriendly'. It's really a case of 'user stupid'.

Fax machines are also taking the sting out of blind dates. Many romances are sparked by the mellow tones of a voice on the other end of the phone. But before falling for the wooing words and to avoid being seen with a nerd on the night, insist upon him faxing his face first.

Like it or not, the Age of the Mainframe is here to stay. Go slowly, don't push it. Take one day at a time. Start simply. For instance, learn to use the remote control on the television. Next month, you might feel you can move along and attempt to master the answering machine. (Mona Mann had enormous problems grasping the concept of this device, always addressing the machine as if it were a third person, i.e. 'Tell Colette her mother rang!')

A course on 'How to Read a Manual' could be an advantage for those still feeling a little technologically timid. The pace is up to you. Go for it! Because, to quote Milton Berle: 'We owe a lot to Thomas Edison —if it wasn't for him, we'd be watching television by candlelight'.

*L*ove in the suds

Soap opera junkies and proud of it

Now that the Human Rights Commission has been established, equal pay for equal work is well under way, and the cause of Animal Liberation is gaining momentum, it is now time for the group who have been oppressed and subjugated into secrecy to step out of the closet and *stand up for soap*.

For too long, we of the gentler sex have been made to feel of substandard intelligence because of our soft spot for viewing the soaps. Because of this prevailing attitude, on many occasions we have been forced to adopt covert and sometimes downright weird practices in order to pursue our harmless habit.

One member of our clandestine society has actually admitted that she has been compelled at times to watch her beloved programme crouched in front of the television set with the sound reduced to such a level that it's barely audible. She was driven to this extraordinary behaviour for fear of alerting the neighbours to her addiction.

Another fellow of our group relates an equally sad

story. As usual, she had settled in to watch her favourite daytime soap, 'Another World', when suddenly she was interrupted by a knock at the backdoor. It was the electrician; he had returned unexpectedly to check on some loose wiring. Realising she'd been discovered, and feeling panic-stricken, she covered herself by saying 'Oh, I wonder who turned that on?', desperately hoping he wasn't aware she lived alone.

We could go on for pages with similar stories we have uncovered about the depth of the discrimination our group has suffered over the years, but suffice to say a change in this situation is not only opportune but vital.

Now, for all you Doubting Thomases out there who have been known to question the integrity of this daytime obsession, we implore you to reserve your judgment. Don't cast your vote hastily until you have heard our theory on the positive side of the world according to soaps.

Apart from the oasis of relaxation it provides in the desert of your average day, the viewing of soap provides you with a wealth of information on a variety of subjects. Massive amounts of bizarre knowledge can be gleaned by the discerning watcher in subjects as diverse as the effect of sniffing ancient Egyptian mummy dust in twentieth-century middle America to what to wear *après* plane crash on a Caribbean island while *en route* to the Paris showing of your designer collection.

No subject is considered too daunting for a soap opera storyline. They cover it all: medical knowledge, fashion and lifestyle, crime fighting (both amateur and professional), the law, and the old backbone to every good soapie worth its suds, the realm of human relationships.

On the theme of things medical, one example of the knowledge that can be gained is limitless insight into the twilight zone of comas. No self-respecting soap is complete without someone in a comatose condition. It has been known to wreak enormous change, not the least of all being its effect on the physical appearance of the particularly drowsy patient. 'Santa Barbara's' C. C. Capwell was rendered unconscious by the sight of his then-wife Gina in bed with his eldest (and none too popular at the best of times) son, Mason, getting together in the biblical sense. C. C. suffered a stroke on the spot and for many weeks was hooked up to a machine that went 'beep, beep, beep'. During his convalescence, his face receded further and further into the bed-clothes until he disappeared entirely, only to re-emerge many weeks later, completely recovered, looking like an entirely different person vaguely resembling Don Craig from 'Days of Our Lives'.

Not all comas are of this magnitude. 'Another World's' Sam Blake's catatonic experience was remarkable for its brevity. As a struggling young artist, Sam was having to drive a taxi to support his pregnant wife, Amanda. It was dark, it was raining, a child ran onto the road, Sam swerved, hit a tree, and the next thing you knew, he was hooked up to a machine going 'beep, beep, beep'. Things were not looking too good. He might have died, but if he did live, the threat of a blood clot blurring his vision was looming. However, he did come good, Amanda looked a bit fuzzy... and all this in just one episode.

The most common consequence for soap opera patients in this stupefied state is that, on regaining consciousness, they suffer a bout of memory loss. Mac and Rachel Cory had a shocking time trying to remember who they were in 'Another World' after inadvertently sticking their noses into an urn of ancient Egyptian mummy dust.

Paralysis (hysterical or otherwise) is another very popular medical condition. Thankfully, this is never a permanent state for our daytime heroes. After the obligatory term in a hospital bed, 'beep, beep, beep', or wheelchair, some traumatic incident gets that adrenalin flowing again, and they are up on those legs and off!

See what you've learned so far?

The education in fashion and lifestyle afforded to you by the soaps is invaluable. Whether our anguished idols live in Genoa City, Salem, Los Angeles, Bay City, or Santa Barbara, their income, regardless of their employment, allows them to wear the latest in designer gear every day. Although never actually seen at the hairdresser's, their coiffures are always perfect. Steve 'Patch' Johnson has spent the past sixty 'Days of Our Lives' on the run from the law—he didn't do it—but has still managed to keep his tresses clean, streaked, moussed and blow-dried. There is a lot to be learned from this man!

You will also learn that buffet breakfasts and beaded blouses are big. If you're lucky enough to view an episode which combines the two, it's mind-blowing. How many of us would know the correct way to eat Special K while dressed in an ultramarine sequinned gown with cowl neckline? Our superstars of the suds know, and are seen to do it regularly. Of course, it helps tremendously if you have a Bridget, a Mamie, an Esther, or some sort of Mamacita, to do the dirty work for you so as to avoid a major meltdown of the beaded frock in the heat of the kitchen.

Another sphere of enlightenment for the television spectator is the territory of fighting crime. According to the soaps, you don't even have to be a member of a police force to engage in this activity. There's a little bit of sleuth in us all! Whether it be a serial killer on the rampage, a rapist with a mother complex, a kidnapper specialising in ten-year-olds, or a manipulative patriarch who dabbles in criminal projects of all kinds, everybody gets involved.

Two popular exponents of this amateur detection were Felicia Gallant and that midget mate of hers, Wallingford, as they raced about 'Another World', involving themselves in everybody else's danger and usually hindering the professionals. On the other hand, in 'Days of Our Lives', Bo and Hope Brady were so adept at fighting crime that they were elevated from their amateur status and invited to turn professional.

On the pro circuit, there are some top-level operators. It was hard to go past Larry Ewing and M. J. McKinnon for pure bloodhound excellence. However, problems loomed in 'Another World' when M. J.'s aim grew shaky with her lust for Larry. She left Bay City while Larry, with all the other little Ewings, vanished without explanation. They have now been replaced by super gumshoe, Adam Cory, and his psychic offsider, Lisa.

The professional crimebusters always work in pairs, but for the citizens of Salem in 'Days of Our Lives', they have an extraordinary situation: detective Roman Brady comes as his own pair. Roman I was wounded and kept frozen on a slab for many years by evil patriarch, Stefano DiMeara. Later, he was brought back to life, given extensive cosmetic surgery, and returned to Salem as Roman II. He continues to fight evil to this day.

But for us the bee's knees, when it comes to pursuers of lawbreakers, has to be 'Santa Barbara's' Cruz Castillo. This man is a paragon. He never sleeps. Whether it be dawn, dusk, day or night, you can count on him if a crime is committed. Cruz Castillo is always on the case—even while contending with a personal life that would make Susan Renouf's story look positively lacklustre.

The rounding up of evil-doers often results in an incredibly long and drawn out court case. This situation is very useful in soaps because it allows every man and his dog to participate and give evidence, whether or not they were anywhere near when the crime was committed—and, besides, it's a great excuse for some more fab outfits.

Apart from what to wear to court, we also learn a lot about the Law. As the accused in the soaps is invariably innocent, we can safely assume that if we were ever tried for murder, we would just have to drag out the trial long enough for some conscience-stricken individual to jump to his or her feet with a climactic confession of guilt!

The vast expanse of human relationships, and the handling of same, is of such enormity we just can't do it justice within the limitations of this chapter. However, suffice it to say that no-one is very happy for very long in a soap opera. There is no love without conflict, whether real or imagined. The list of star-crossed lovers has no end—young, old or middle-aged; sick, dying or paralysed; blonde, brunette or redhead; thin, thin, or thin—no-one is safe from the ravages of an interminably tempestuous liaison.

Some outstanding examples of this recurring theme in soaps are Bo and Hope Brady from 'Days of Our Lives', Victor and Nikki Newman from 'The Young and the Restless', Mac and Rachel Cory from 'Another World', Cruz and Eden Castillo from 'Santa Barbara', and the most indestructible coupling of all, Tom and Alice Horton from 'Days of Our Lives', who've been at it for almost thirty years. And, of course, let us not forget 'General Hospital's' Nurse Jessie—she's been married to everybody!

Seeing how these outrageous relationships can be applied to our day-to-day lives may be a little confusing. But therein lies the answer. It doesn't matter how bad things are for us. One quick look at the three-ring circus our soap idols continually find themselves in, makes any of our situations look brighter immediately.

Well, there you have it, warts and all. This is our stand for soap. Choose for yourselves, but feel safe in the knowledge that if you do decide to join in the fun, you won't be alone! To heighten your pleasure even more, here is a final tip—do it with a friend! There is nothing quite like settling down with your best mate, a chunk of iced carrot cake in one hand, a hot mug of tea in the other, amidst the comfort of your favourite soap's theme music. It caresses your senses. It's heaven!

WARNING

PERSONS SENSITIVE TO SEXUALLY EXPLICIT MATERIAL
SHOULD NOT TURN THIS PAGE
SHOULD NOT READ THIS CHAPTER
SHOULD NOT SHOW ANYONE THIS PASSAGE
SHOULD NOT PASS 'GO'
SHOULD NOT COLLECT $200.

27

*A*re you ripe for sex in the nineties?

A comprehensive quiz to help assess your sensuality

After extensive research on the subject of sex, both in theory and in practice, we have designed this quiz to guide you in your approach to erotic satisfaction as the world spins off its lascivious axis into the next century.

1 After a few sensuality-heightening circuits with your partner on a merry-go-round, and then walking home with your arms entwined while sharing a Blue Heaven ice-cream, you find your arousal meter is at nooky point. Do you make love:
    (a) with all the lights on?
    (b) in complete darkness?
    (c) in the glow of a flickering fire?

2 The long, lingering come-hither looks across the sea of computer terminals, coupled with the occasional tantalising touch of bare skin over a shared straw dispenser in the canteen, have finally proven fruitful and he is coming for dinner tonight. Do you greet him at the door in:

(a) a fur bikini?
(b) a see-through nylon peignoir?
(c) a simple cotton shift?

3 It's been a great party, a real rage. You've had a smidge too much to drink and you're worried about driving home alone. Scanning the room for a suitable companion for the long trek, you keep in mind the possibility that he may become a breakfast partner. Do you then choose:
(a) a mysterious stranger?
(b) a good friend of fifteen years?
(c) an ex-boyfriend, recently returned from overseas?

4 You are about to embark on a new and, hopefully, exciting intimate relationship. As it has been quite some time since your last copulatory experience, you fear that your carnal abilities may be a little rusty. Do you then:
(a) read *The Joy of Sex*?
(b) thumb through the *Kama Sutra*?
(c) rely on your memory?

5 You've met his parents, you've watched his kid brother play football, you've been invited to be his sister's bridesmaid, so now things are looking really serious. You plan an intimate dinner for the two of you in the hope he will pop the question. Do you serve:
(a) eels in port wine?
(b) a roast dinner?
(c) a takeaway pizza?

6 You find yourself alone one night, and now that you have survived the sexual revolution and emerged as a liberated being (coitally speaking that is), you can take responsibility for your own pleasure. Do you use:
(a) a battery-driven plastic vibrator?
(b) a cucumber?
(c) a strong water jet?

7 While attending a Self-realisation Course, you feel something hard pressed against your thigh during the Hugging Seminar. Your eyes lock, and instantly you

both know to quit the course and head for the nearest motel. A method of contraception is needed quickly. Do you:
- (a) dust off the old diaphragm in your handbag?
- (b) ask him to use a condom?
- (c) chance it with coitus interruptus?

8 Your once highly titillating relationship has hit a bit of a rough patch—you feel the shagging is lagging. While listening to 'Sex Talkback' on midnight radio, you hear that the use of aphrodisiacs is recommended as a must for your lust. Do you use:
- (a) powdered rhinoceros horn?
- (b) peaches?
- (c) amyl nitrate?

9 Your sexual maturity is at such a peak that you feel confident enough to talk to your partner about what 'bits' you like best and what you like done to your 'bits'. When stating your preference of position for The Act, do you demand:
- (a) the missionary position, while tied to a four-poster bed?
- (b) doggie-fashion, on your hands and knees?
- (c) standing up, face to face, in an open field?

Now go to the next page to reveal the answers to this quiz and discover if you are sexually ripe enough to enter the nineties.

ANSWERS

Question 1
(a) 0—This may be exciting for you, but it does nothing for the energy crisis.
(b) 10—This may be dreary, but thank you for being so ecologically aware!
(c) 0—Very soap opera, very romantic, but let's quit burning the fossil fuels.

Question 2
(a) 0—You may think you look cute, but what about the endangered species' life you ended?
(b) 0—Most alluring and we understand works a treat, but who wants a man-made fibre against their skin?
(c) 10—You're nature's girl in that natural look!

Question 3
(a) 10—Yes, as long as you practise safe sex, keep your jeans on, and don't put your head under in the spa!
(b) 0—Good friends can be boring at breakfast.
(c) 0—You never know where this one has been.

Question 4
(a) 0—You read it before, and it didn't help then.
(b) 0—Not much use since the back gave way.
(c) 10—Good on you; no paper needed for this answer, you've just saved two trees in the Amazon forest!

Question 5
(a) 10—Good choice: with eel being a recognised aphrodisiac, he'll soon be popping more than the question!
(b) 0—No good; will remind him of Sundays at his mother's.
(c) 0—No good; will remind him of every other day of the week.

Question 6
(a) 0—A technological nightmare made of unrecyclable material and battery acid.
(b) 10—A real green alternative and can be safely sub-

stituted by a zucchini or a green bean, depending on your size preference!

(c) 0—With the people on the land suffering from drought, do you really think this is fair?

Question 7

(a) 0—Too long in the handbag; has probably had any number of cosmetics spilt on it, rendering it unsafe.

(b) 0—This is only a possibility in the event of the recyclable condom being invented.

(c) 10—As far as we are aware, this does not offend any concerned single-issue group and has been known to give lovemaking a real edge!

Question 8

(a) 0—It's people like you that have the rhinoceros cowering in its cave and hanging on to its horn.

(b) 10—As long as it is organically grown, this fruit is perfect, as the sweet juices are symbolic of the secretions of the female genital organs!

(c) 0—In the short term maybe, but eventually recreational drugs are so unsatisfactory.

Question 9

(a) 0—Slavery went out with Abraham Lincoln, and if he's got to tie you up to keep you there, what's the point?

(b) 0—This form of oppression should be taken for a walk. Suggest a pet.

(c) 10—Freedom, equality and spiritual enlightenment are embodied in this position, and by standing up, you give the flora and the fauna a fair go, too!

If you scored between 70 and 90, congratulate yourself. You are ripe for sex in the nineties and eminently beddable. Apart from being acutely aware of the ecological problems facing the world today, you display an ingenuity and intelligence that we admire. Let's do lunch!

If you scored between 40 and 60, don't despair. You're still in there with a chance. You've got some maturing to do. Obviously, you are still clinging to some of your eighties' standards and have yet to be fully enlightened to the joys of ecologically aware congress.

If you scored between 0 and 30, it's time to take a really good look at yourself. We're not living in the seventies now. Pack away your tired old fur bikini and get that dried flower arrangement out of your hair. It's time for you to move on—the sooner the better!

To be really ripe for sex in the nineties, make sure your G-spot is a Green Spot!

The Nineties Woman

Now let's see who's been paying attention!

Fill in the blank spaces in the following statements:

1 When accepting a blind _____ , the Nineties Woman will always use her _____ machine and insist that he fax his _____ first.
2 To avoid that _____ feeling, the Nineties Woman would definitely _____ him first.
3 For the Nineties Woman, life has become one great big _____ -in.
4 In today's corporate world, the Nineties Woman and her _____ pads cannot do without _____ .
5 When planning a party, the Nineties Woman never forgets to organise her _____ game, Get _____ .
6 Noticing her man is parting his _____ on the other side, the Nineties Woman renews her _____ membership.
7 When complaining to her building supervisor, the Nineties Woman always does it with _____ and never in her _____ .

8 The Nineties Woman does need a _____ to know that the word 'Canberra' means '_____ breasts'.
9 When watching _____ opera, the Nineties Woman is not intimidated by Ridge Forrester's _____ .
10 The Nineties Woman is in tune with her need for _____ sex, and therefore supports research into _____ able condoms.
11 When confronting her girlfriend's _____ head husband, the Nineties Woman retains her _____ and _____ and bears it.
12 For an aphrodisiac, the Nineties Woman knows the value of a good _____ and how dangerous _____ horn can be.
13 When travelling, the Nineties Woman knows to put her husband and children into the family _____ and book herself a _____ in _____ class.
14 At funerals, family or otherwise, the Nineties Woman abhors the taking of _____ of _____ bodies.
15 The Nineties Woman knows her way around a _____ -room and can capitalise on a deserting husband's feelings of _____ .
16 In the _____ place, the Nineties Woman can tell the difference between a hard _____ or a floppy _____ in her boss's office.
17 In the gym, the _____ Woman can recognise that a big _____ size does not necessarily mean a healthy _____ .
18 When voting at an election, the Nineties Woman knows that _____ is cheap and is not easily swayed by Italian _____ , big _____ , or weeping _____ .
19 Environmentally speaking, the Nineties _____ is acutely aware of her _____ -spot and knows what colour it is— _____ .
20 As a sexual being, the Nineties Woman is _____ sound, practises _____ sex and uses a _____ for her own _____ .

29

A survival register

What every Nineties Woman needs to have on hand

As we wend on our womanly way to the end of this century, it has become apparent to us that certain necessities are imperative for our continuing survival. This is our register of suggestions for your consideration, but bear in mind that this is just a guide. Alterations and adjustments according to your own particular whims are more than acceptable. As a matter of fact, they are encouraged.

1. Enough money to always fly first class.
2. A personal fitness trainer, preferably male and cute.
3. A nanny or a nanna, or both, for the Nineties Mum.
4. A builder's licence, or the equivalent—and better still, in a very small pair of shorts.
5. A best girlfriend who is immune to the charms and charisma of dickheads.
6. A 34-inch television screen.
7. A good cause.
8. Frequent access to an alien.

9 A make-up and hair stylist for all photographic occasions.
10 A partner-for-life who has no relatives at all.
11 The latest, up-to-the-minute gas hot water system.
12 A crate of peaches.
13 A fax machine to avoid the blind-date nerd.
14 An obstetrician with a sense of humour and who does not look like Sweeney Todd.
15 A personally customised supermarket trolley without a dicky wheel.
16 A permanent booking in an isolation ward every Christmas.
17 A devoted husband much younger than you.
18 A reinforced steel bull-bar for legally breaking into lines of trafic.
19 A thesaurus—so much better than a dictionary when writing your book.
20 A girlfriend to lunch with, shop with, exercise with, watch soap operas with, travel with, be pregnant with, recycle with, plan parties with, talk money with, and write a book with.